Essential Music Theory

8

Mark Sarnecki

San Marco Publications

Essential Music Theory © 2022 by San Marco Publications. All rights reserved.

All right reserved. No part of this book may be reproduced in any form or by electronic or mechanical means including Information storage and retrieval systems without permission in writing from the author.

ISNB: 9781896499333

Contents

Lesson 1: **Clefs**	1
Lesson 2: **Scales**	5
Lesson 3: **Modes**	14
Lesson 4: **Melody 1**	21
Lesson 5: **History 1**	28
Review 1	32
Lesson 6: **Intervals**	35
Lesson 7: **Time**	41
Lesson 8: **Triads**	54
Lesson 9: **Seventh Chords**	62
Lesson 10: **Cadences**	68
Lesson 11: **Melody 2**	83
Lesson 12: **History 2**	88
Review 2	90
Lesson 13: **Transposition**	93
Lesson 14: **Score Types**	101
Lesson 15: **Melody 3**	114
Lesson 16: **History 3**	118
Review 3	121
Lesson 17: **Form and Analysis**	124
Music Terms and Signs	130
Exam	138

1
Clefs

Why do we use different clefs? Wouldn't it be easier just to use one clef? To understand why we need different clefs look at **Figure 1.1** and 1.2. Figure 1.1 is a melody in the treble clef. If we wanted to write this melody in the bass clef as shown in Figure 1.2, we would have to use a lot of ledger line notes, and they can be hard to read. Different clefs allow the notes to stay on and around the staff and make the music easier to read.

Figure 1.1

Figure 1.2

C Clefs

A *C clef* establishes the location of the note C on the staff. This is middle C on the piano. Wherever the little notch in the center of the clef occurs is where middle C is located. **Figure 1.3** is a C clef with middle C on the third line.

Figure 1.3

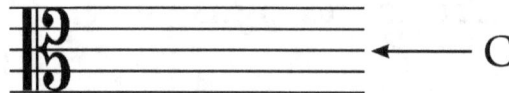

The C clef is different than other clefs because it is a *movable clef*. Depending on which line the clef indicates, the name is different. The C clef can be placed on various lines of the staff.

Figure 1.4 shows four different C clefs. We will study the alto and tenor clef.

Figure 1.4

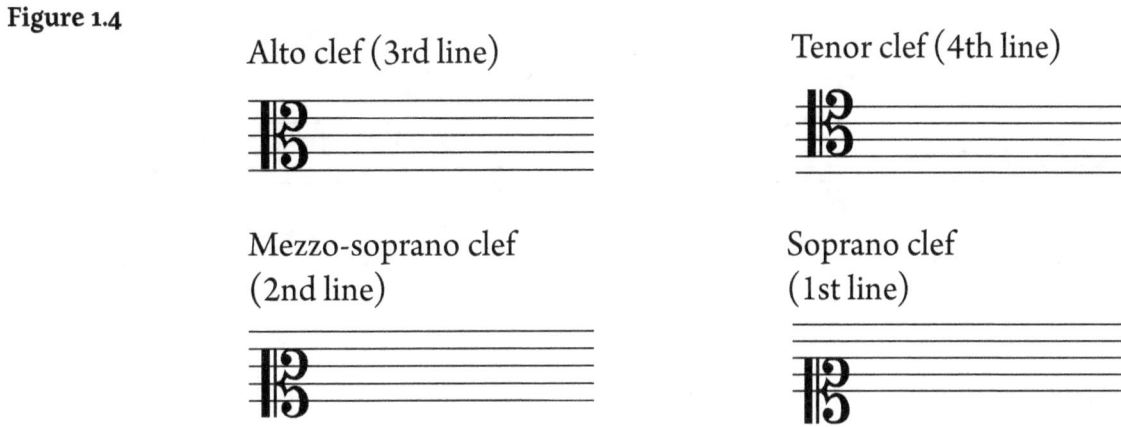

The Alto and Tenor Clef

The *alto clef* is used by the viola and the *tenor clef* is used by the 'cello, trombone, and bassoon. Other C clefs are not used today. **Figure 1.5** shows the alto and tenor staves with notes.

Figure 1.5

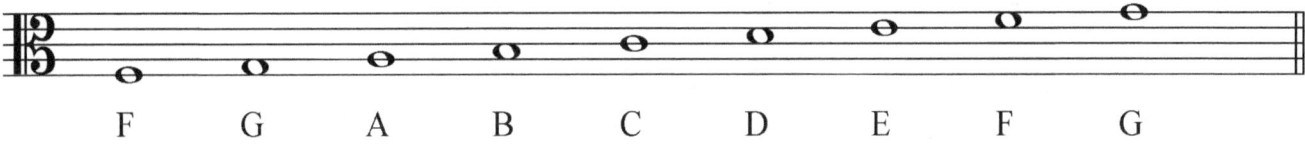

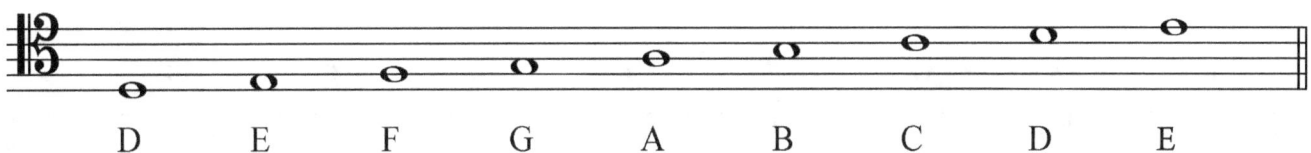

1. Name the following notes.

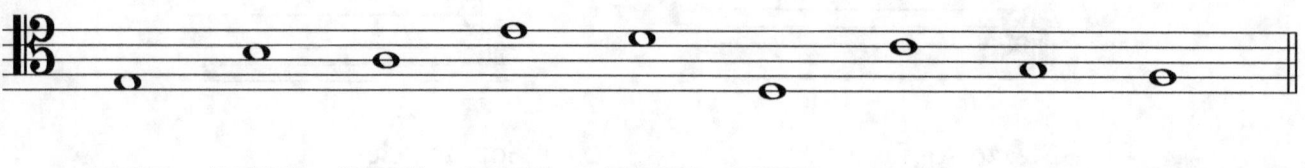

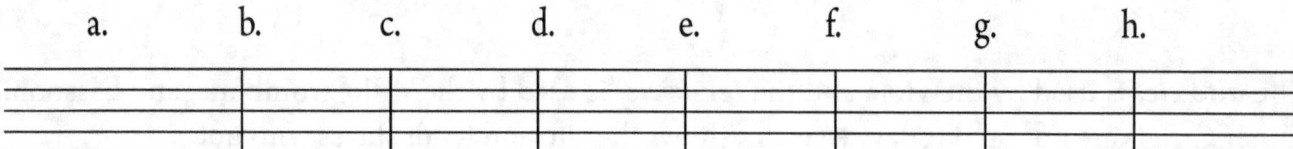

2. Draw an alto clef and write the following notes.

        a. E on a line   e. middle C
        b. B in a space   f. D on a line
        c. D in a space   g. E in a space
        d. F on a line   h. A in a space

a.   b.   c.   d.   e.   f.   g.   h.

3. Draw a tenor clef and write the following notes.

        a. middle C   e. G in a space
        b. D in a space   f. D on a line
        c. E in a space   g. B in a space
        d. F on a line   h. A on a line

a.   b.   c.   d.   e.   f.   g.   h.

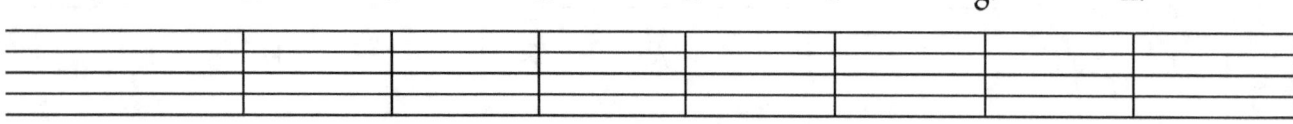

4. Rewrite the following passage using the alto clef.

Wolfgang Amadeus Mozart
Cosi fan tutte

5. Rewrite the following passage using the tenor clef.

Gabriel Faure
Elegie, Op. 24

2
Scales

Review - The Circle of Fifths

The *circle of 5ths* is a chart organizing all of the keys into a system that we can use to relate them to one another. Each key in the circle is separated by the interval of a perfect 5th.

In **Figure 2.1** minor keys are shown with lower case letters.

Figure 2.1

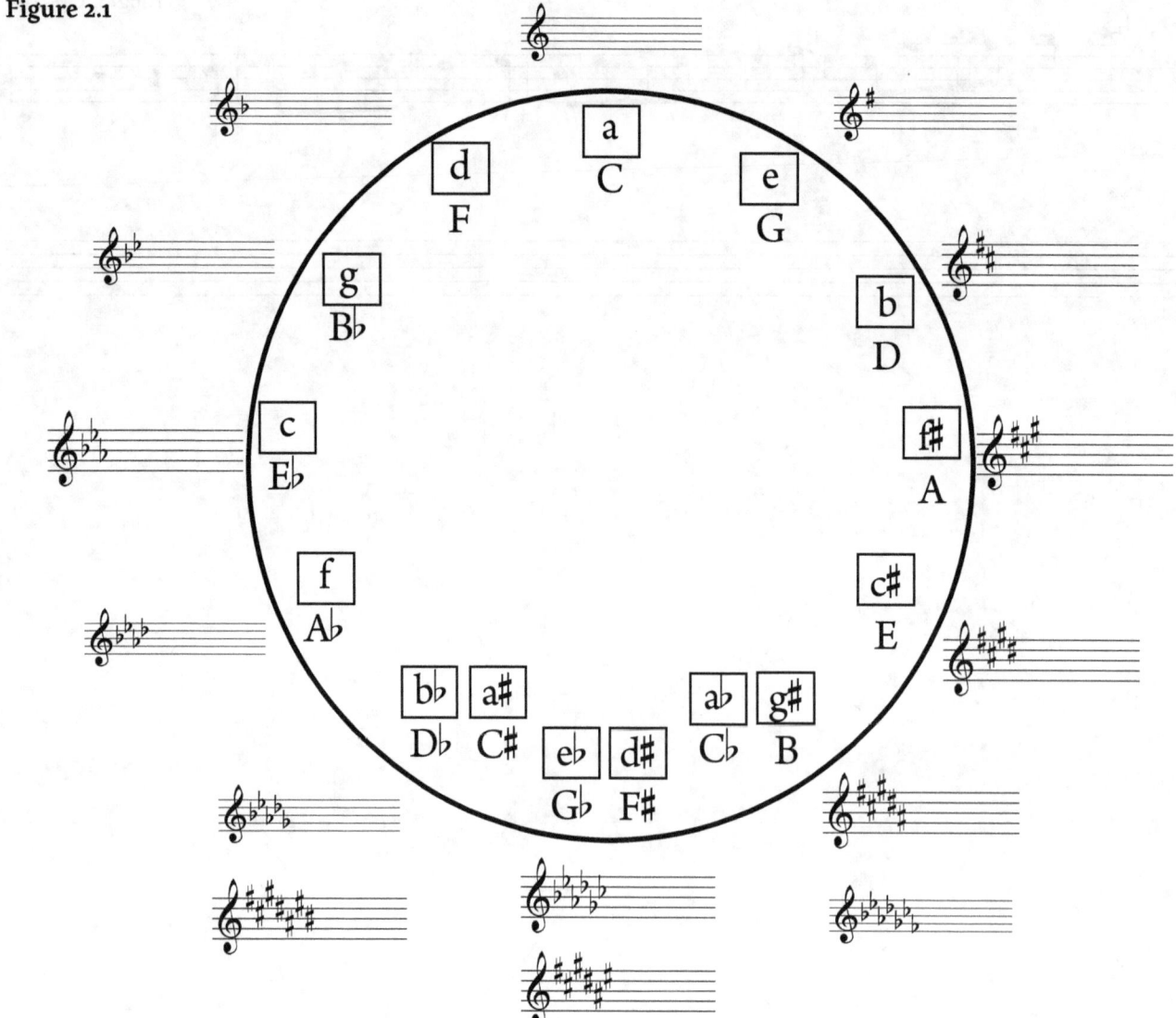

Key Signatures

The sharps or flats in a key signature always appear in a specific order. The order of the sharps is:

F C G D A E B

C major has no sharps or flats. **Figure 2.2** is a list of the sharp keys and their location on the staff.

Figure 2.2

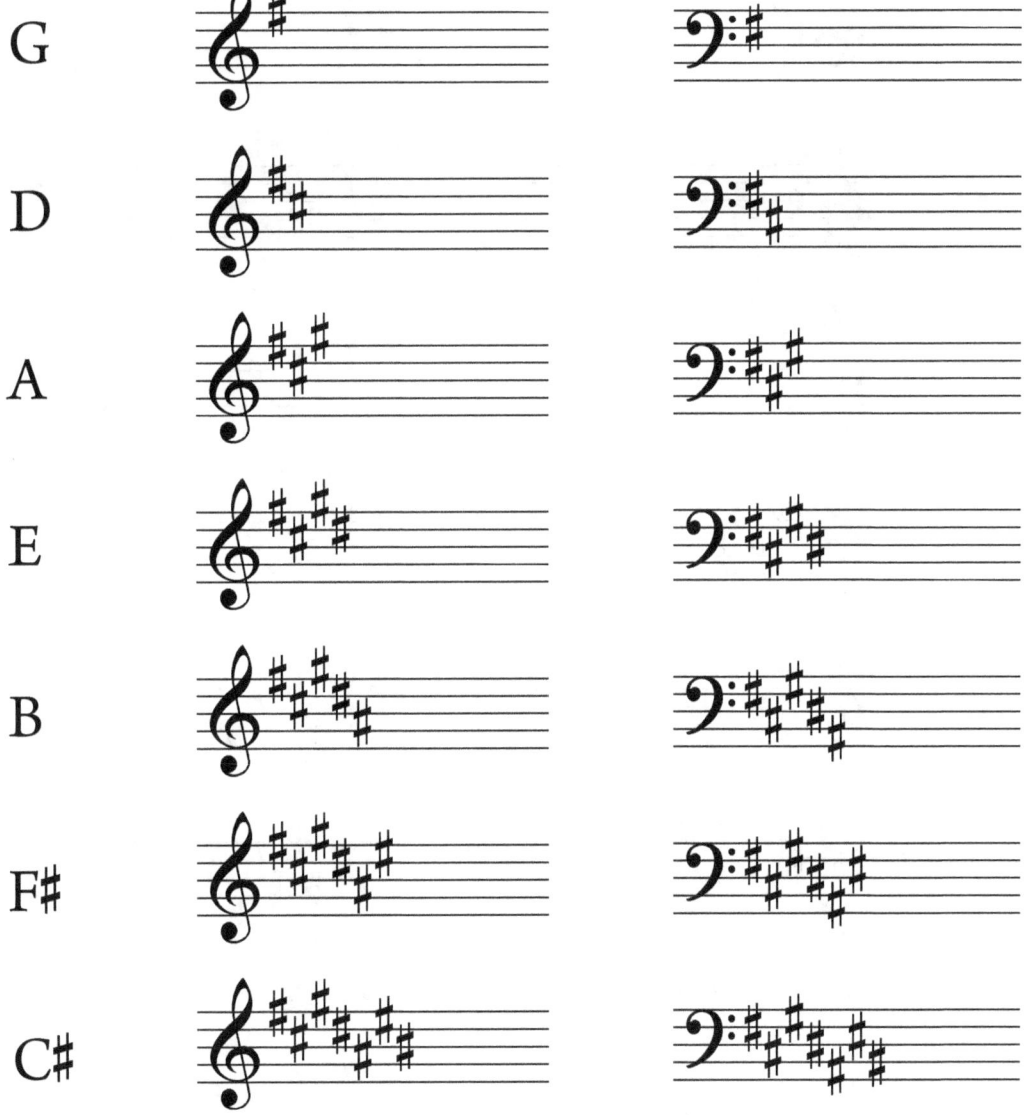

The order of the flats in a key signature is:

B E A D G C F

Figure 2.3. is a list of the flat keys and their location on the staff.

Figure 2.3

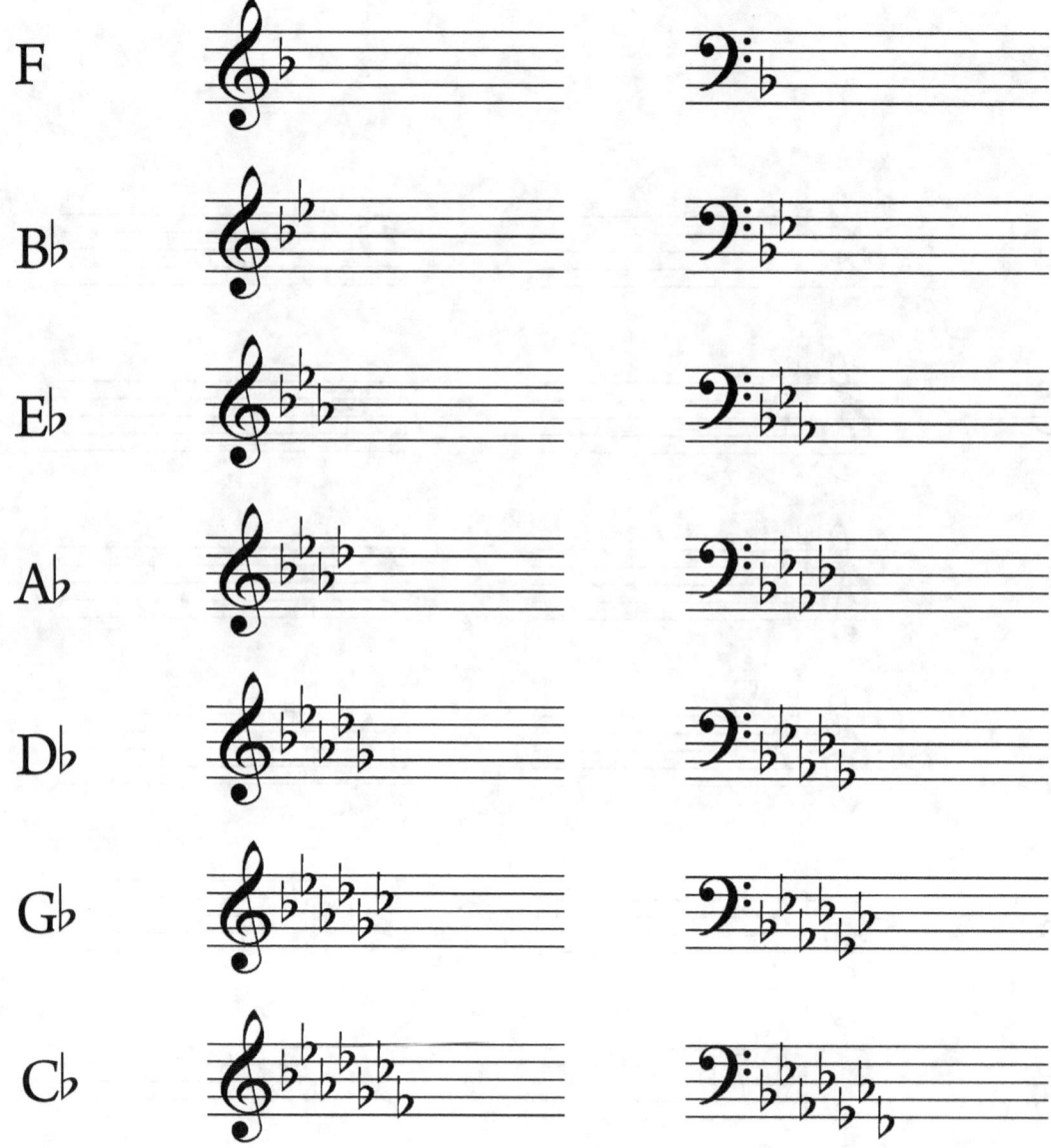

Key Signatures in the Alto and Tenor Clef

Figure 2.4 illustrates the placement of sharps and flats on the alto and tenor staff.

Figure 2.4

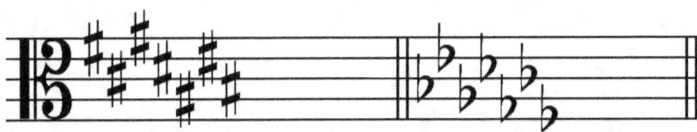

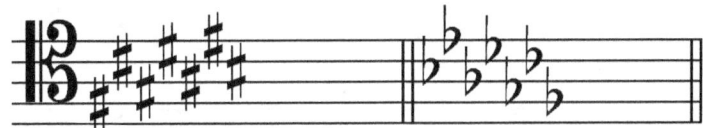

1. Write the following key signatures in the alto clef.

| D major | G minor | F minor | A major | E♭ major | B major |

| C♯ major | B♭ minor | E minor | C♭ major | G♭ major | F♯ major |

2. Write the following key signatures in the tenor clef.

| G major | C minor | F♯ minor | E major | D♭ major | D major |

| B major | B minor | C♯ minor | C♯ major | C♭ major | E♭ minor |

Scale Review

The Major Scale - all major scales are based on the following pattern of whole and half steps.

whole -whole- half-whole-whole-whole half

C major scale

The Natural Minor Scale - the natural minor scale uses the same key signature as its relative major. The relative minor of C major is A minor.

A natural minor scale

The Harmonic Minor Scale - the harmonic minor is formed by raising scale degree $\hat{7}$ of the natural minor scale one half step ascending and descending.

A harmonic minor scale

The Melodic Minor Scale - the melodic minor is formed by raising scale degrees $\hat{6}$ and $\hat{7}$ of the natural minor scale one half step ascending and lowering them one half step descending.

A melodic minor scale

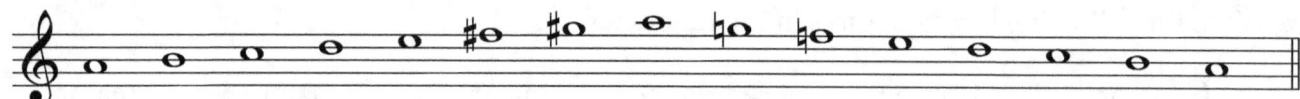

The Chromatic Scale - the chromatic scale consists of semitones. It is often written with sharps ascending and flats descending.

C chromatic scale

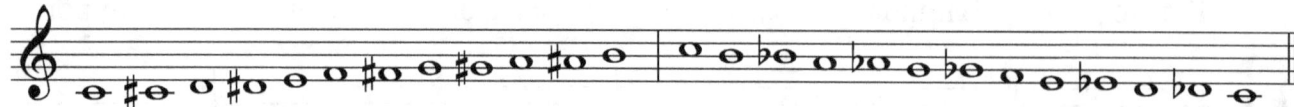

©San Marco Publications 2022 — Scales

The Whole Tone Scale - the whole tone scale consists of whole tones. Every whole tone scale contains the interval of a diminished 3rd.

C whole tone scale

The Major Pentatonic Scale - the major pentatonic scale can be formed by removing scale degrees $\hat{4}$ and $\hat{7}$ from a major scale. The C major pentatonic scale is: C D E G A C.

C major pentatonic scale

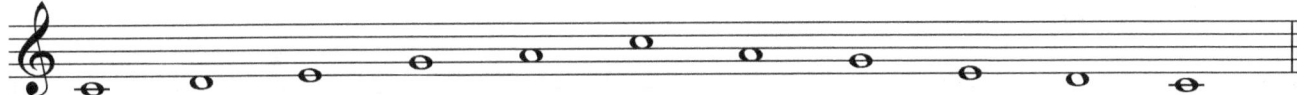

The Minor Pentatonic Scale - the minor pentatonic scale can be formed by removing scale degrees $\hat{2}$ and $\hat{6}$ from a natural minor scale. The A minor pentatonic scale is: A C D E G A.

A minor pentatonic scale

The Blues Scale - the blues scale is the major scale with $\hat{3}$, $\hat{5}$ and $\hat{7}$ lowered a half step. $\hat{5}$ occurs twice, once lowered and once in its original form. Scale degrees $\hat{2}$ and $\hat{6}$ are omitted.

A blues scale

The Octatonic Scale - the octatonic scale, sometimes called the diminished scale consists of alternating whole and half steps. There are two varieties: One starts with a whole step, and one with a half step.

C octatonic scale

1. Add the correct clef and necessary accidentals to form the following scales.

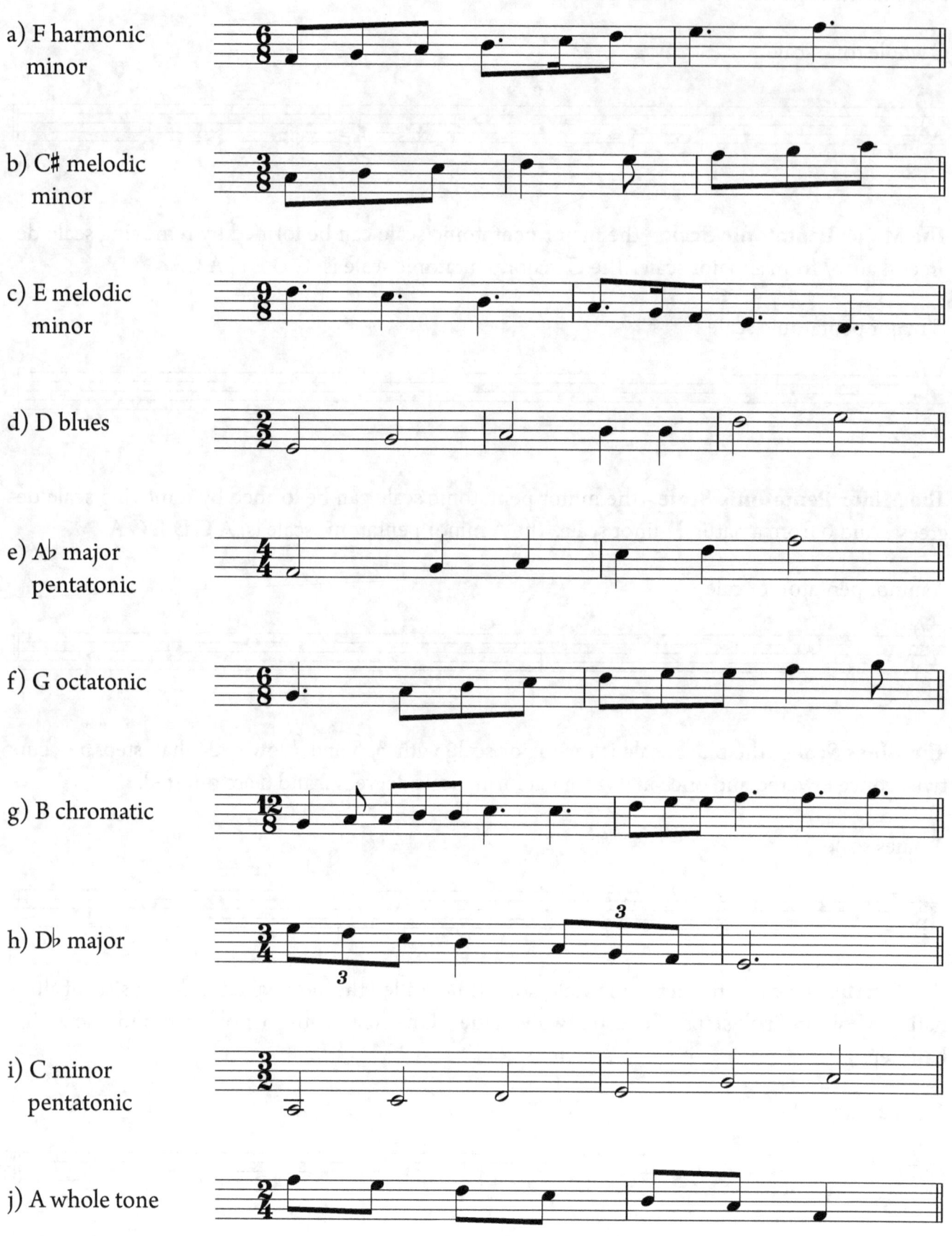

You may be asked to write a scale starting on a note other than the tonic. In this case, take care when writing a minor scale and raising or lowering $\hat{6}$ and $\hat{7}$. If you start on a note other than the tonic, these two notes will be in a different place within the scale. **Figure 2.5** contains the D melodic minor scale starting on the dominant ($\hat{5}$). Scale degrees $\hat{6}$ and $\hat{7}$ become the second and third notes in this scale.

Figure 2.5

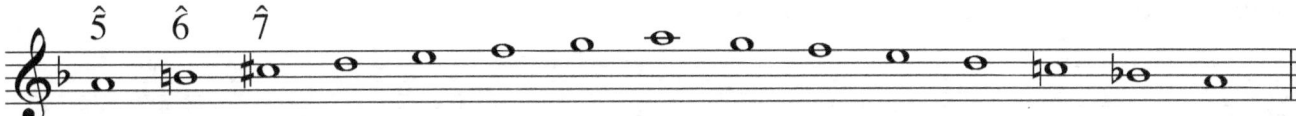

1. Write the following scales ascending and descending using a key signature for each.

E major from mediant to mediant

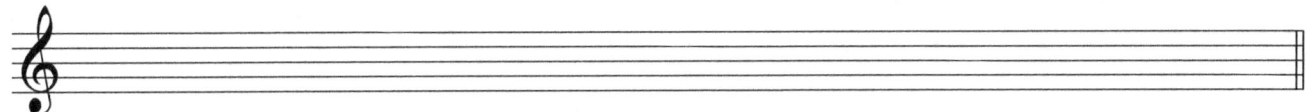

F# harmonic minor from supertonic to supertonic

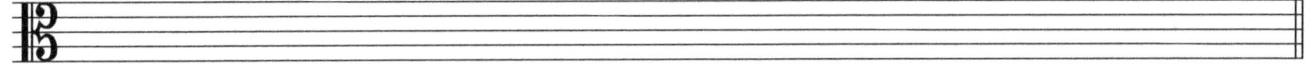

E♭ melodic minor from submediant to submediant

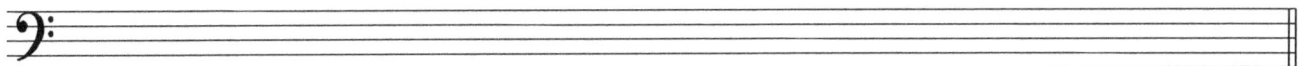

B major from subdominant to subdominant

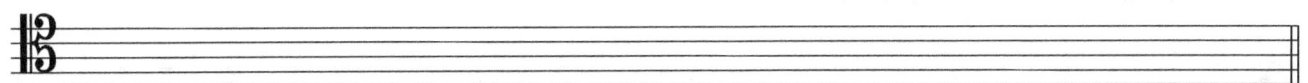

G harmonic minor from submediant to submediant

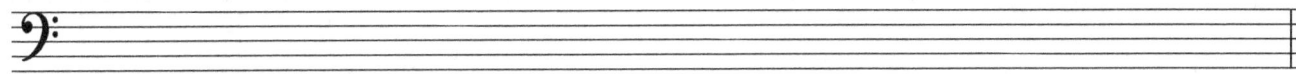

2. Write the following scales ascending and descending using a key signature for each.

G♭ major

G♭ major's enharmonic tonic minor, harmonic form

E♭ major

E♭ major's relative minor, melodic form

G♯ melodic minor

B♭ major

B♭ major's parallel minor, harmonic form

C♯ natural minor

3
Modes

A *mode* is a type of scale. Modes are also called "church modes" because they were originally used by the Catholic church in Medieval times. Modes were used to compose the melodies of Gregorian chant and remained in use throughout the Middle Ages. With the rise of the major and minor tonal system in the Baroque era, modes were rarely used in the Baroque, Classical, and the majority of the Romantic eras. They were revived by the Impressionist composers and are used most frequently today by rock and jazz players in improvisation and composition.

There are seven modal scales. Each major scale can be approached from seven different angles with one mode starting from each note of the scale. We will examine each mode using the key of C.

Ionian

The **Ionian mode** is the same as the **major scale**. All the white keys on the piano from C to C. It has the same patterns of whole and half steps as the major scale. It is used in all Western music from classical to rap. **Figure 3.1** is the C Ionian mode.

Figure 3.1

Dorian

The **Dorian mode** begins on the 2nd degree of the major scale. Using the scale of C it goes from D to D. **This is the same as a natural minor scale with raised $\hat{6}$.** This mode is used in rock, jazz, blues and fusion music. **Figure 3.2** is the D Dorian mode.

Figure 3.2

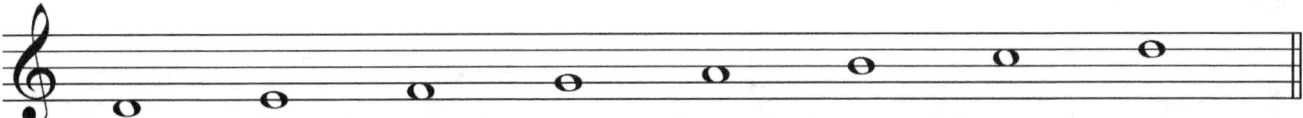

Phrygian

The ***Phrygian mode*** begins on the 3rd degree of the major scale. Using the scale of C, it goes from E to E. **This is the same as a natural minor with lowered $\hat{2}$.** This mode has a Spanish sound and is used in Flamenco and fusion music. **Figure 3.3** is the E Phrygian mode.

Figure 3.3

Lydian

The ***Lydian mode*** begins on the 4th degree of the major scale. Using the scale of C, it goes from F to F. **This is the same as a major scale with raised $\hat{4}$.** This mode is used in country, rock, jazz, blues and fusion music. **Figure 3.4** is the F Lydian mode.

Figure 3.4

Mixolydian

The ***Mixolydian mode*** begins on the 5th degree of the major scale. Using the scale of C, it goes from G to G. **This is the same as a major scale with lowered $\hat{7}$.** This mode is used in rockabilly, country, rock, and blues music. **Figure 3.5** is the G Mixolydian mode.

Figure 3.5

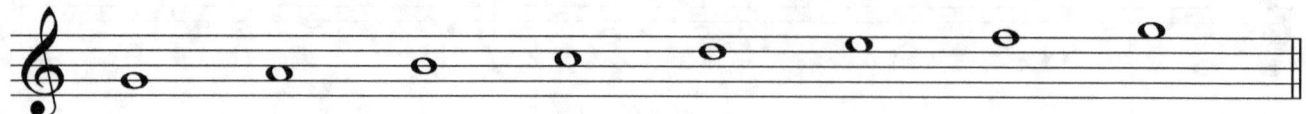

Aeolian

The ***Aeolian mode*** begins on the 6th degree of the major scale. **This mode is also the natural minor scale.** Using the scale of C, it goes from A to A. It is used in most music including pop, country, rock, jazz, blues, classical, hip-hop, rap, etc. **Figure 3.6** is the A Aeolian mode.

Figure 3.6

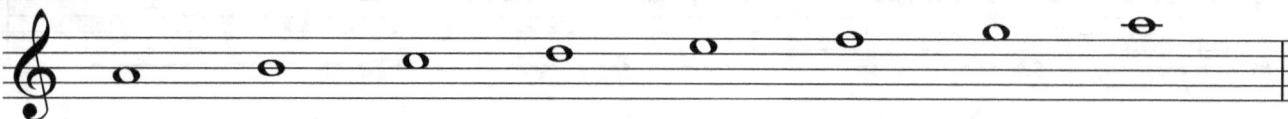

Locrian

The **Locrian mode** begins on the 7th degree of the major scale. Using the scale of C, it goes from B to B. **This is the same as a natural minor scale with lowered $\hat{2}$ and lowered $\hat{5}$.** It is the least commonly used mode but can be found in some jazz and fusion music. **Figure 3.7** is the B Locrian mode.

Figure 3.7

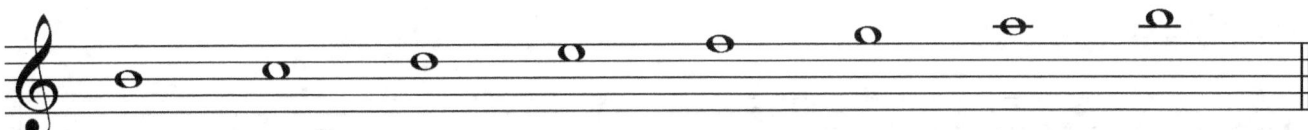

Writing Modes

When writing modes, it is helpful know their order. Here is a saying to help you remember the order of modes: *I Don't Punch Like Muhammad Ali.*

Let's say we are asked to write the B♭ dorian mode.

1. First, the dorian mode starts on $\hat{2}$ of a major scale.
2. Determine what major scale has B♭ as scale degree $\hat{2}$, (A♭ major).
3. Write the mode from B♭ to B♭ using the key signature of A♭ major (4 flats).
4. You're done! See Figure 3.8.

Figure 3.8

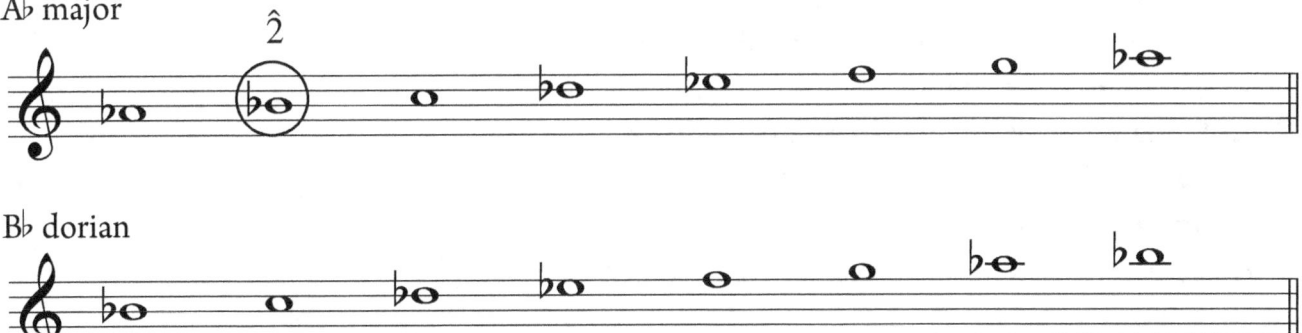

To write the A mixolydian mode.

1. The mixolydian mode starts on $\hat{5}$ of a major scale.
2. Determine what major scale has A as scale degree $\hat{5}$, (D major).
3. Write the mode from A to A using the 2 sharps of D major (F♯ and C♯).
4. Modes use accidentals. See Figure 3.9.

Figure 3.9

D major

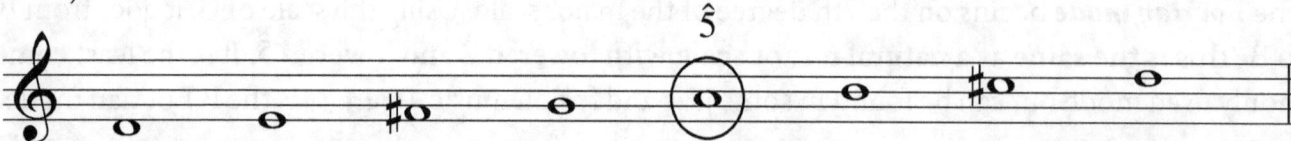

A mixolydian

Another Way to Look at Modes - An Easier Way!

There is an important aspect to understand about modes. Even though modes look like they are derived from notes within a major scale, you should learn and know the modes as their own entities. For example, the G Mixolydian mode (G-A-B-C-D-E-F-G) looks a lot like the traditional G major scale (G-A-B-C-D-E-F#-G). The only difference is the G Mixolydian mode contains an F♮, and the G major scale contains an F#. You could look at this mode as an altered type of major scale. In other words, a major scale with a lowered $\hat{7}$.

Looking at modes as comparable to most major or minor scales can make them easier to understand. Here is a list of the modes and how they relate to major and minor scales.

1. **Ionian**   is the major scale
2. **Dorian**   is a natural minor scale with a raised $\hat{6}$
3. **Phrygian**   is a natural minor scale with a lowered $\hat{2}$
4. **Lydian**   is a major scale with a raised $\hat{4}$
5. **Mixolydian** is a major scale with a lowered $\hat{7}$
6. **Aeolian**   is the natural minor scale
7. **Locrian**   is a natural minor scale with lowered $\hat{2}$ and $\hat{5}$

It can help to remember the modes using the above method. In this way, you can learn them as distinct scales and write and identify them easily. For example, if you wanted to write the A Dorian mode, you would just write an A natural minor scale with a raised $\hat{6}$ (F#).

Figure 3.10

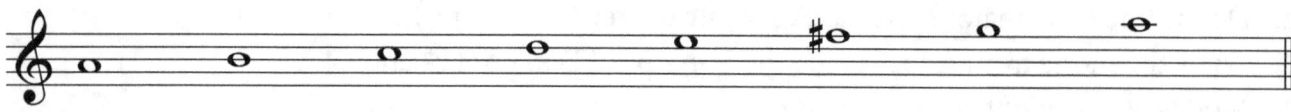

A dorian

1. Write the following modes ascending using accidentals instead of a key signature.

C lydian

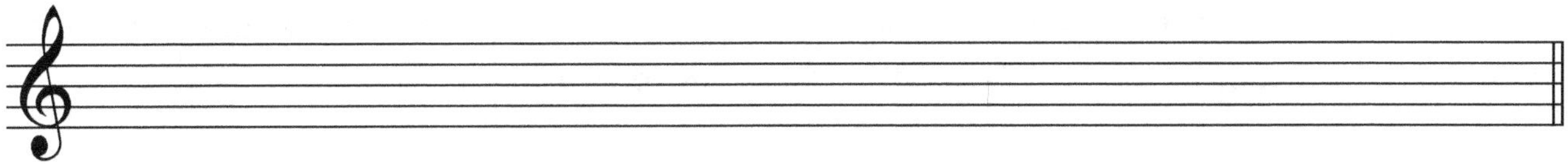

G phrygian

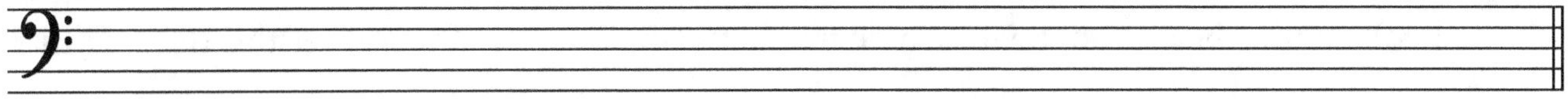

E mixolydian

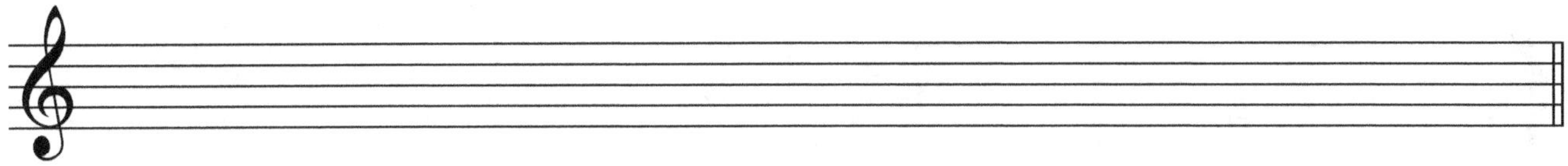

C dorian

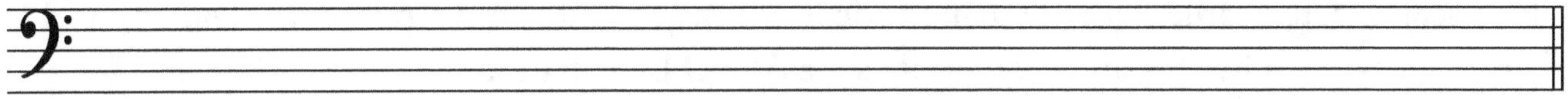

D aeolian

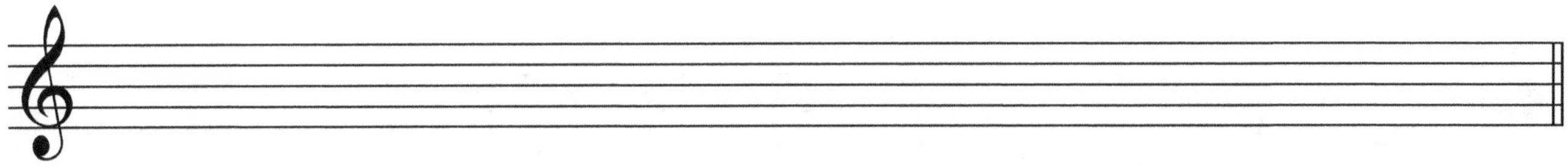

F locrian

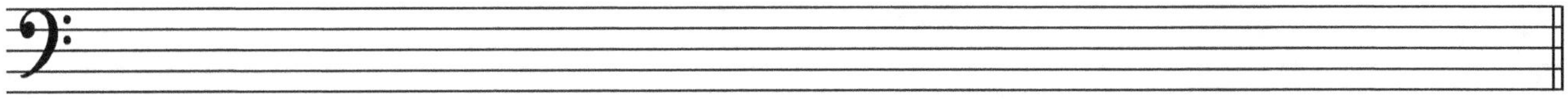

E♭ lydian

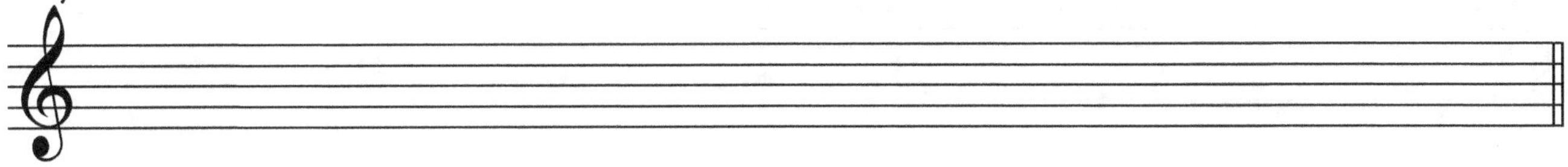

F♯ mixolydian

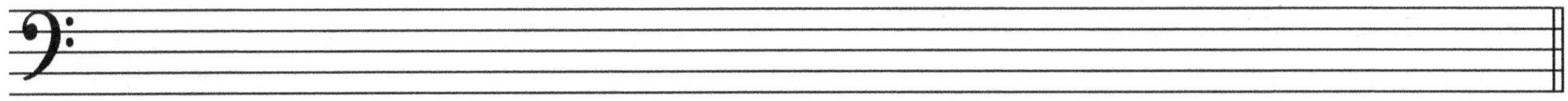

©San Marco Publications 2022   Modes

Identifying Modes

It is fairly simple to identify a mode. One way is to know the order of the modes, and on what degree of the major scale they occur. To identify the mode in **Figure 3.11**:

1. Collect the accidentals to determine the major scale. Here, there are three sharps indicating the scale of A major.
2. What is the starting note of the mode? Here it is D. D is the fourth note of the A major scale.
3. The Lydian mode begins on the fourth degree of the major scale. That makes this the D Lydian mode.

Figure 3.11

Modes can also be identified easily if you know the relationship between modes and the major and minor scales stated earlier. The Lydian mode is the major scale with a raised $\hat{4}$. **Figure 3.11** is a D major scale with a G♯. This quickly identifies it as the D Lydian mode.

1. Identify the following modes.

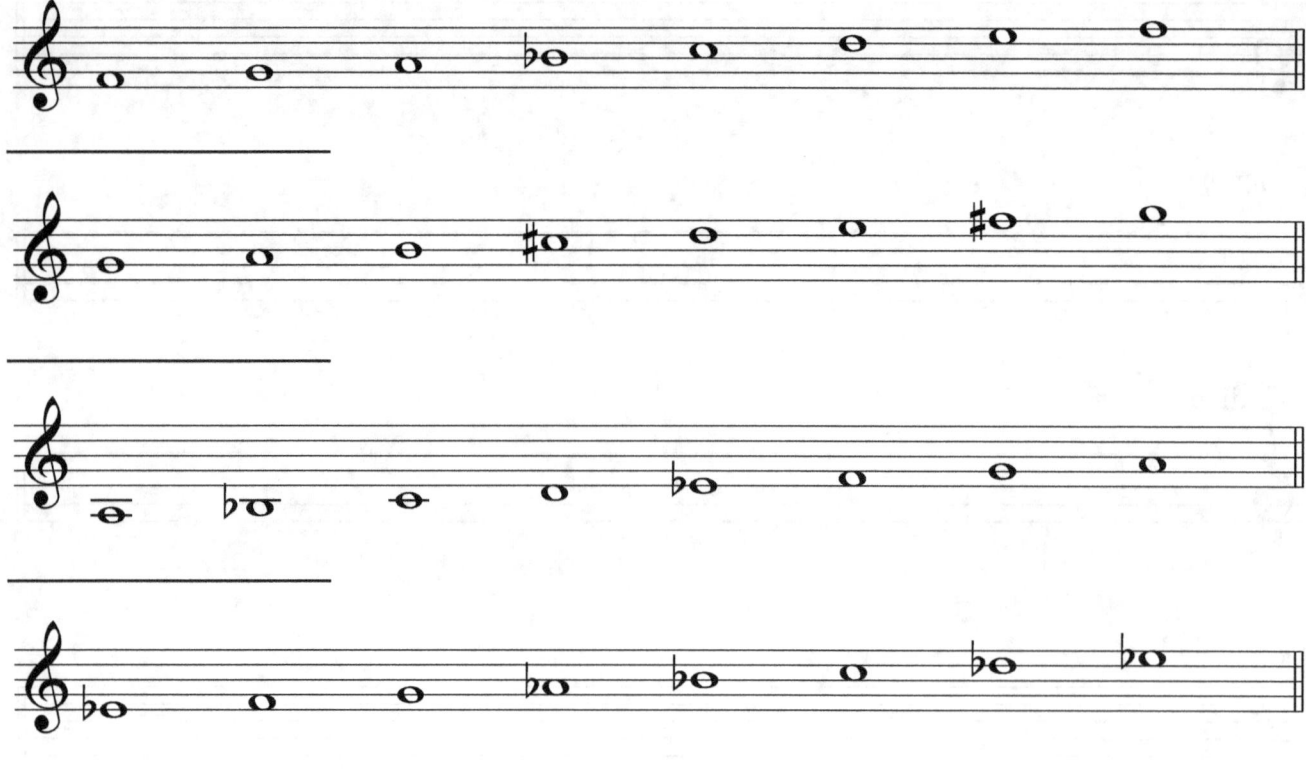

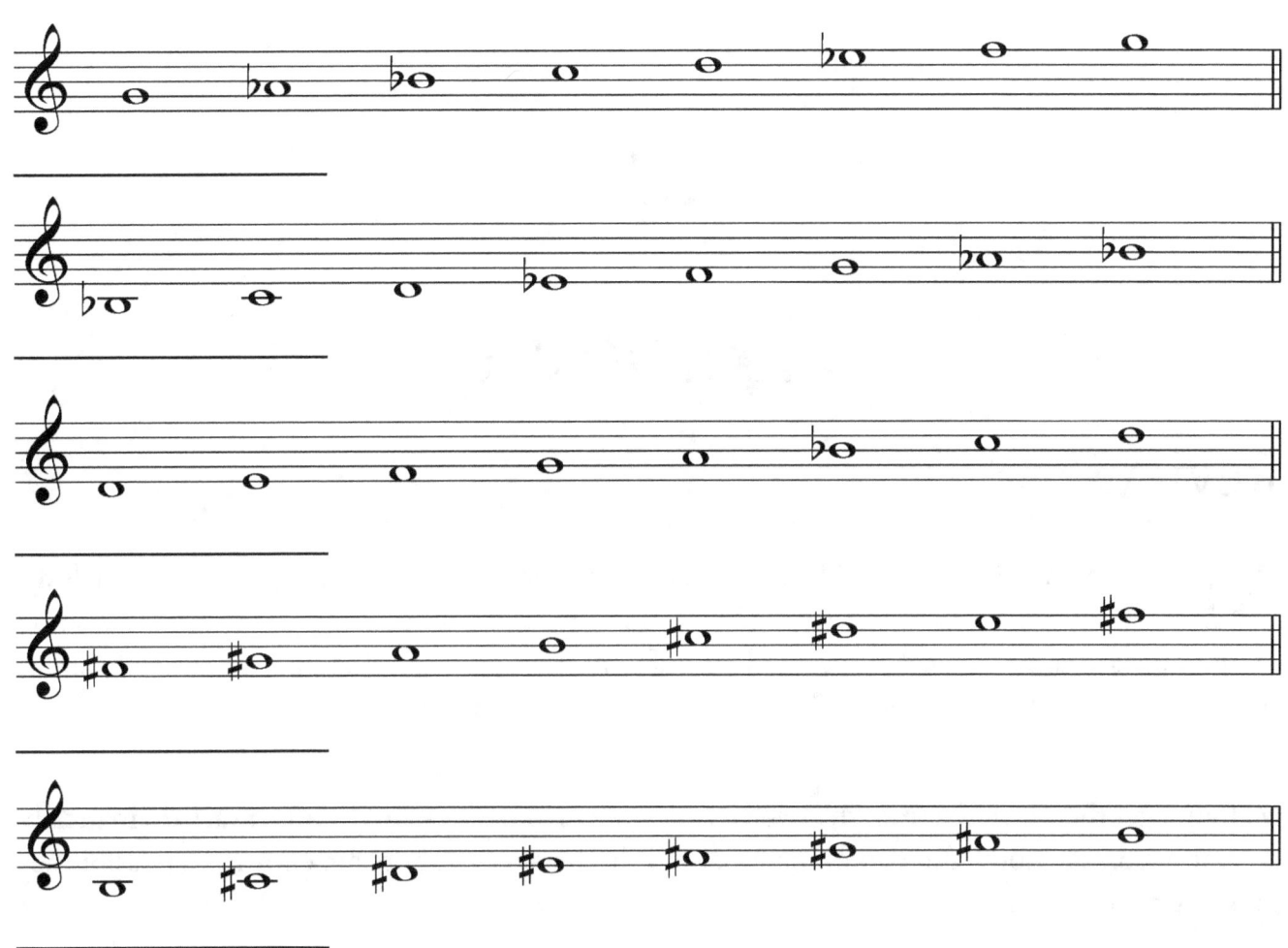

4
Melody 1

Review

Music is made up of many different elements, but one of the most recognizable is melody. A melody is a musical gesture made up of individual, connected pitches. It could also be thought of as a single musical line. Melody is different from harmony, in that a melody is heard as single notes, one after the other, while harmony features more than one note sounding at the same time.

Melodies get their material from the twelve-note system of pitches, but they can vary dramatically depending on the notes, their combinations, and rhythms used. There are enormous possibilities for creating melodies.

The notes of a melody may move in various ways. The melody is **Figure 4.1** moves mostly by step. Stepwise movement is known as ***conjunct motion***. Stepwise motion gives a melody flow and makes it very singable.

Figure 4.1

Ludwig van Beethoven
Symphony No. 9, IV

A *leap* is the interval of a 3rd or larger. The melody in **Figure 4.2** moves mostly by leap. Movement by leap is known as ***disjunct motion***. Leaps add interest and energy to a melody.

Figure 4.2

Anonymous
Minuet BWV 116

Most melodies are a mixture of steps, leaps, and repeated notes. The melody in **Figure 4.3** combines all of these elements.

Figure 4.3

Christian Petzold
Minuet BWV 114

Melodic Contour

The motion between individual notes gives a melody *contour*. Contour determines what makes a melody memorable and expressive. When one note moves to another, it can repeat, move up or down, or it can move by step or by leap.

There are five possible combinations of these movements, so there are five basic types of melodic motion. A melody can move up by step, down by step, up by leap, down by leap, or repeat.

It's the combination of these five types of motion that give a melody its contour. We can visualize the contour of a melody as a long line or ribbon. This line gives us information about the melody's balance between up, down, step, leap, and repeat.

The example in **Figure 4.4** a) has a wavy line that is created by leaps, steps, and directional changes. **Figure 4.4** b) is a classic arched melody that moves to a high point in the phrase (climax), and then returns downward. Both are effective.

Figure 4.4

Extreme melodic shapes are not always suitable. A spiky, harsh shape occurs when a melody has too many large leaps. **Figure 4.5** contains a melody with too many large leaps, resulting in a disjunct, unmusical melody.

Figure 4.5

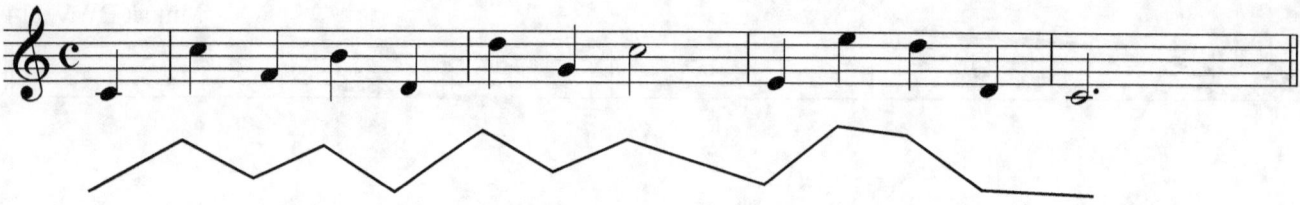

The melody in **Figure 4.6** circles around the same few notes. This results in an uninteresting, flat shape. Try to avoid this type of melody.

Figure 4.6

Understanding contour helps us understand what makes melodies memorable and expressive. Good melodies tend to have diverse contours; that is, they tend to make balanced use of all different types of melodic motion. These types of melodies may use all five types of melodic motion in each phrase. An effective melody will often contain opposite pairs of motion such as a leap followed by a step, ascending notes followed by descending notes, or both.

Writing Melodic Leaps

Stepwise motion in a melody is good, but like anything, too much can make a melody boring. Leaps within a melody can add drama and interest, but they must be treated carefully. The following information is a general guideline to help you create effective melodies. However, occasional exceptions may be found in musical literature.

- Don't write more than three leaps in the same direction. Too many leaps may create an excessively large range and affect the shape of a melody. The melody in **Figure 4.7** contains three ascending leaps and then it changes direction.

Figure 4.7

The melody in **Figure 4.8** has six leaps in a row covering two octaves. This is a considerable range and not very effective especially if you have to sing it.

Figure 4.8

- More than one leap in a row in the same direction sounds like a broken chord. When writing more than one leap up or down, be sure that they combine to outline a recognizable chord or harmony. Study the melody in **Figure 4.9** which contains efficient leaps outlining specific chords within the key.

Figure 4.9

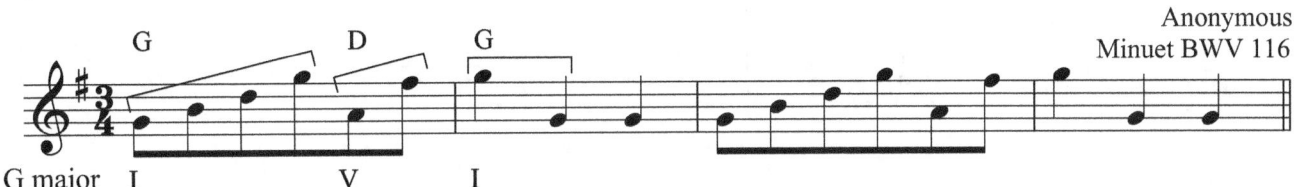

The melody in **Figure 4.10** contains leaps that are poor. The leaps in m.1 are good because they outline the tonic triad. The leaps in m.3 do not outline a recognizable chord in G major. Not only are they bad, but they sound bad as well. This type of consecutive leap should be avoided.

Figure 4.10

1. Name the keys and put brackets on the consecutive leaps in the following melodies. Add a ✓ on the correct leaps, and an ✗ on the incorrect leaps.

- It is best to approach a large leap (a 6th or more) with a note from within the leap. This is a note that occurs between the two notes of the leap. The leap in **Figure 4.11** a) works well because it is approached by a note that is found within it. **Figure 4.11** b) is poor because the note of approach is not within the notes of the leap.

Figure 4.11

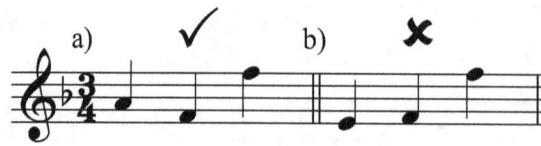

The two downward leaps in **Figure 4.12** work well because they are approached from a note within the leap.

Figure 4.12

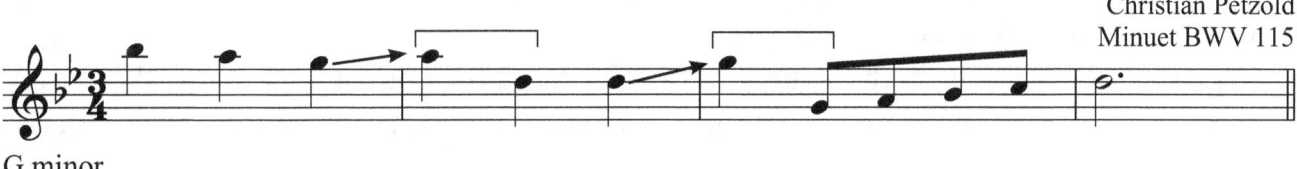

Christian Petzold
Minuet BWV 115

G minor

1. Mark the correctly approached leaps with a ☑ and the incorrectly approached leaps with an ☒ in the following melodies.

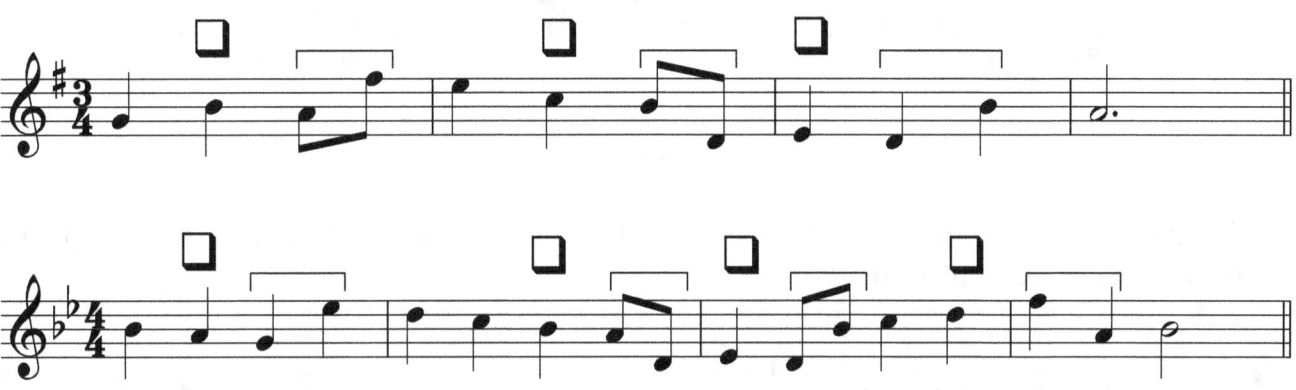

- As a general guideline, it is best to leave a large leap (a 6th or more) by movement in the opposite direction to a note within the leap. There may be occasional exceptions to this when the leap is being followed by a repeated note. In **Figure 4.13** each leap is followed by a note found between the two notes of the leap.

Figure 4.13

Anonymous
Aria BWV 131

- Avoid a leap of a major 7th (**Figure 4.14 a.**). This is an awkward dissonant interval.
- A leap of a minor 7th is fine because it implies a 7th chord (**Figure 4.14 b.**). If you write a minor 7th, it is important to approach it as you approach all large intervals, from a note within the interval. 7ths should be left by step in the opposite direction. A 7th is an interval that requires resolution. This resolution is downward by step.
- When a melody moves in the same direction for more than one note, we hear the interval formed by the first and last notes. Try not to outline an augmented interval or a major 7th (**Figure 4.14c.**)

Figure 4.14

1. Complete the following melodic fragments to create four bar melodies in major keys. End each melody on a stable tone ($\hat{1}$ or $\hat{3}$).

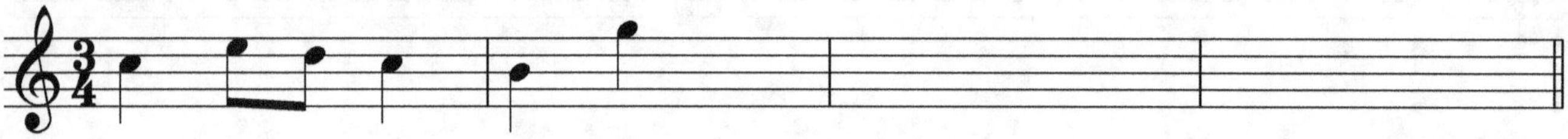

key:_____

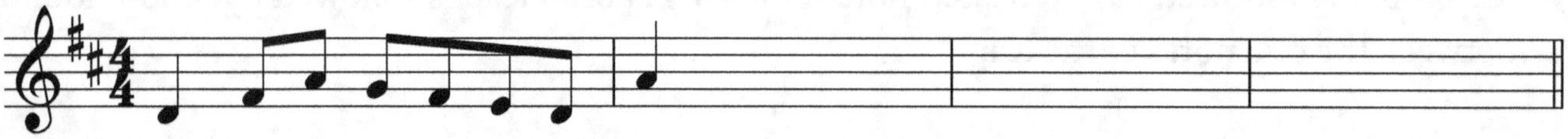

key:_____

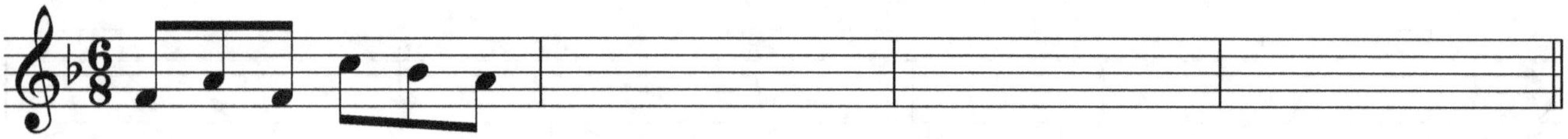

key:_____

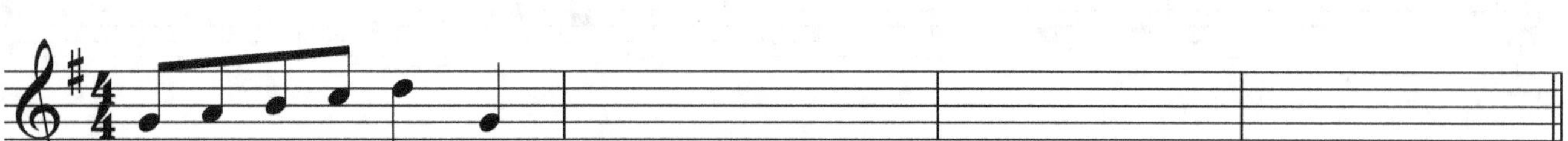

key:_____

©San Marco Publications 2022

5
History 1

The Medieval Era (500- 1450)

The medieval era took place from approximately 500 to 1450 A.D. This was a period of heavy church influence. Music was around before this time and had various developments, but during the medieval era, the use and creation of music was regulated by the church.

The church was the main patron of the arts, including music. Many musicians were trained in the church, and the church had the financial means to buy extravagant items like paper, where eventually music was written down. Our current system of music notation is even rooted in the developments made in the medieval church!

Medieval church music had very specific rules, which included the chanting of prayers. Chanting of this period is called **plainchant** and is sometimes referred to as Gregorian chant since Pope Gregory standardized chant for the liturgy. Plainchant is a single line of modal melody, without a measured rhythm, sung in Latin. Modal refers to ancient scales called **modes**, which were studied in Lesson 3.

Plainchant is **monophonic**, meaning it is one melody without harmony, resulting in just one musical part. **Monophony** is a single melody without accompaniment. Monks would sing the prayer together in unison.

Around the year 900, some simple harmony involving two vocal parts was allowed. This type of simple two-part medieval harmony is called **organum**. The harmony was made in one of two ways:

- Sometimes a drone, or low, continuous note, was sung while the main melody was sung at the same time. Drones are still used in bagpipe music today.
- Other times, the words of the song would be sung on two different pitches at the same time.

Ordo Virtutum - Hildegard von Bingen

One of the greatest composers of the medieval era was ***Hildegard von Bingen.*** Hildegard lived from approximately 1098 to 1179. She was a German nun, mystic, poet, and composer who was known for her visions and prophecies. Hildegard wrote poems about her visions and prophecies and set them to music.

Her music is incredibly melodic for the middle ages. The church had very stringent rules about music, yet she was able to incorporate new and extended musical techniques that still fit under the guidelines of the church. She used a wide range of pitches and leaps that were uncharacteristic for the time. These methods were used to give meaning and musical emphasis to the words she wrote.

Hildegard's most renowned work is a musical play called ***Ordo Virtutum***. Ordo Virtutum (The Play of the Virtues), composed about 1151, is a liturgical drama, known as a ***morality play***. A morality play is a drama designed to teach a moral or lesson. Ordo Virtutum is about the struggle for a human soul between the Virtues and the Devil. The text of this work is in Latin, the language of the Roman Empire, and the official language of the church.

Ordo Virtutum contains 82 different monophonic melodies. All parts are sung in plainchant by women, except that of the Devil. Several notes are sung to each syllable of text. A technique called ***melisma***, which consists of many notes sung to one syllable, is used to emphasize important words. Hildegard based the music on modes, which serve to elicit varied feelings, like withdrawal, happiness, sadness, or serenity. The rhythm is free, with no time signatures or meter. The characters in Ordo Virtutum are:

- The Soul, Anima, sung by a female voice.
- The Virtues (Humility, Hope, Chastity, Innocence, Contempt of the World, Celestial Love, Discipline, Modesty, Mercy, Victory, Discretion, Patience, Knowledge of God, Charity, Fear of God, Obedience, and Faith), sung by 17 solo female voices.
- The chorus of the Prophets and Patriarchs, sung by women.
- The chorus of Souls, sung by women.
- The Devil (a male voice) does not sing, he only yells or grunts. According to Hildegard, the Devil cannot produce divine harmony.

Secular Music in the Medieval Era

By the late medieval era, **secular**, or non-religious music, was becoming extremely popular. Secular music employed some of the developments that were made within the church. Royalty also played a prominent part in musical life, since wealthy people could afford to train musicians and pay composers to write for them.

Minstrels and **troubadours** were two types of musicians that were part of Royal court life. Minstrels were not as refined as troubadours and entertained in other ways, like juggling. Troubadours sang songs of chivalry, courtly love, and travel to faraway lands. Secular songs developed more and more during this period using multiple voices and instruments.

Sumer is Icumen In

Sumer Is Icumen In is a medieval English vocal work composed in the mid-13th century. This piece is a **rota**. Rota is another word for a round or canon. A round consists of at least two voices that sing the same melody with each voice beginning at different times.

The text of Sumer Is Icumen In is in Middle English, and the title translates to 'Summer is Coming.' The composer is unknown. This is a **polyphonic** composition for six voices. **Polyphony** consists of two or more melodies singing together. In this case, it's six!

Sumer Is Icumen In contains a repeated two-part section called a **pes** (foot). A pes is a melodic or rhythmic pattern that repeats over and over. A pes is also known as an **ostinato**. **Figure 5.2** is the four measure pes or ostinato written in modern notation. It is usually sung by two tenors.

Figure 5.2

Figure 5.3 is the complete melody of Sumer Is Icumen In. Rather than being written in one of the modes, which was common in the middle ages, it is in a major key. In modern notation you may see it written in 6/8 or 12/8 time and in any number of keys. This example is in F major. Find a recording of this piece on the internet.

Figure 5.3

Music Terms

Study the following French terms and their meanings.

cédez	yield, slow down
léger	lightly
lentement	slowly
modéré	at a moderate tempo
mouvement	movement, tempo, motion
vite	fast

Review 1

1. Write the following scales ascending and descending using key signatures where applicable.

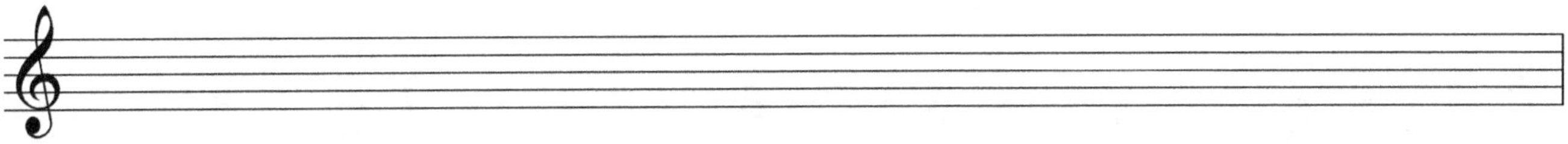

G♭ major

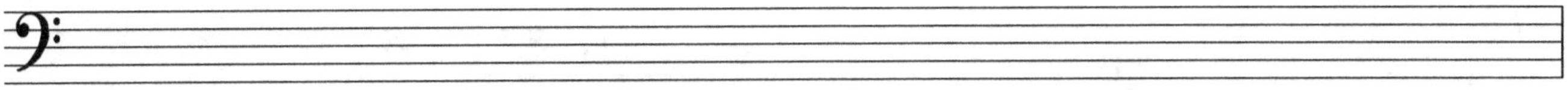

C# minor, harmonic form

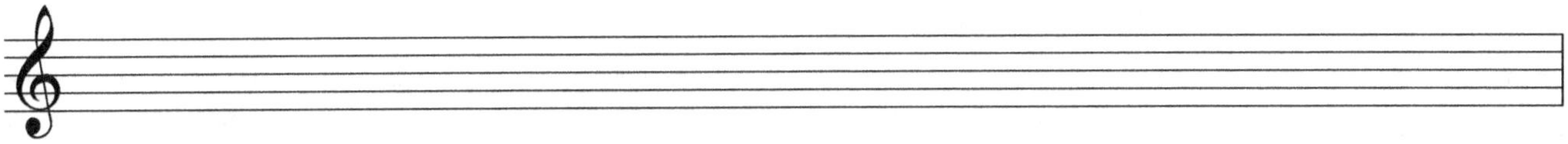

C blues

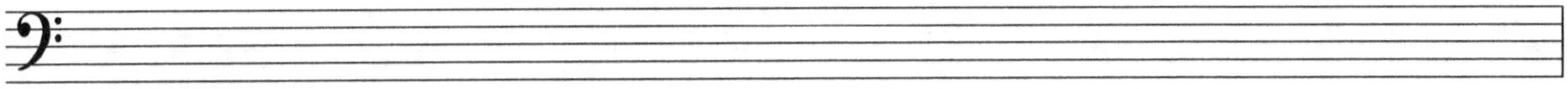

D whole tone

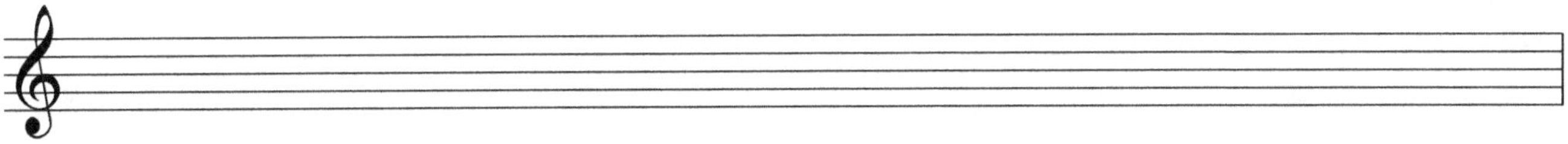

C minor pentatonic

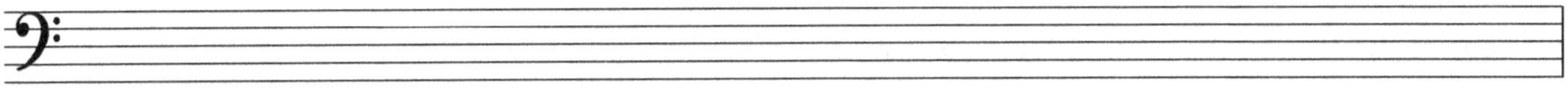

A major pentatonic

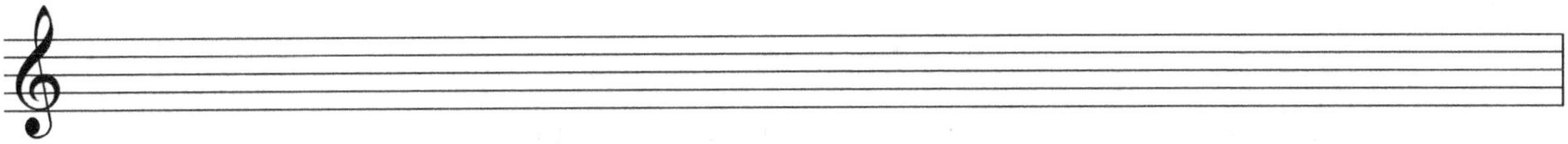

E♭ chromatic

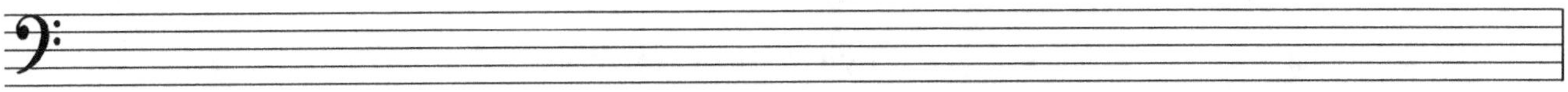

F octatonic

2. Identify the following modes.

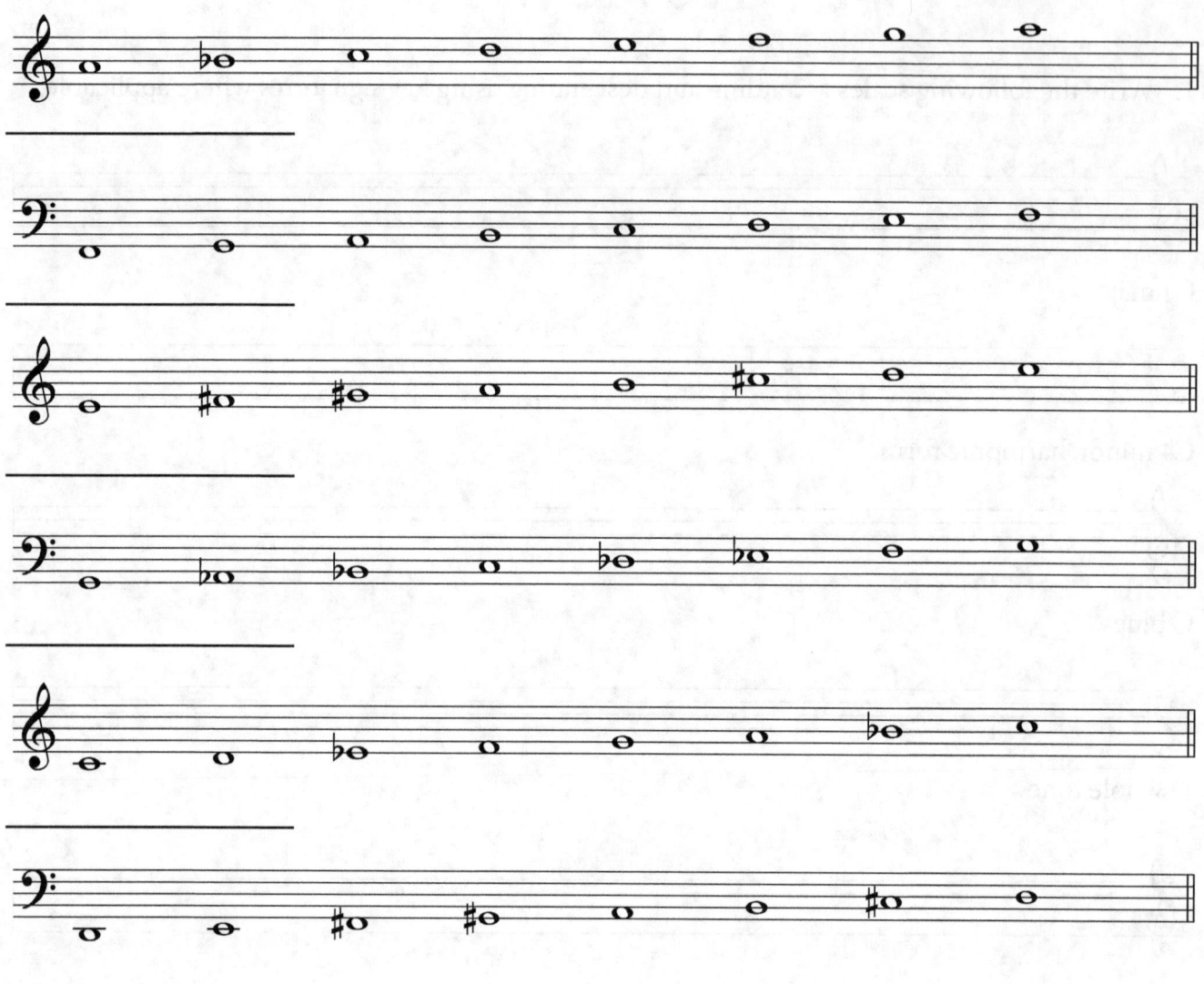

_____

_____

_____

_____

_____

_____

3. Match the following French terms with their meanings.

cédez	_____	a) fast
léger	_____	b) movement, tempo, motion
lentement	_____	c) at a moderate tempo
modéré	_____	d) slowly
mouvement	_____	e) lightly
vite	_____	f) yield, slow down

4. For the following major key melodic fragments: Name the key. Complete the remaining two measures creating a phrase that ends on a stable scale degree (preferably 1̂).

Key:_____

Key:_____

5. State whether the following statements are true or false.

a. The Medieval era occurred during the years ca. 500 - 1650. _____

b. Hildegard von Bingen was a German nun, composer, and mystic. _____

c. *Ordo Virutum* is a morality play. _____

d. A morality play is a genre designed to teach a lesson or moral. _____

e. The text of *Ordo Virtutum* is in Italian. _____

f. Monophony is a single line of unaccompanied melody. _____

g. *Ordo Virtutum* is composed in plainchant. _____

h. Plainchant is an example of polyphony. _____

i. *Sumer Is a Cumen In* is a religious composition. _____

j. *Sumer Is Icumen In* is an example of monphony. _____

k. 'Rota' is another word for 'round.' _____

l. A recurring rhythmic or melodic pattern is known as an *ostinato*. _____

m. A 'Pes" is an 'ostinato.' _____

6
Intervals

Review

An essential part of music theory is understanding the relationship between single notes. The distance between two notes is an *interval*. Intervals form the foundation for practically every concept in music theory.

Major, minor, diminished and augmented are interval *qualities*.

2nds, 3rds, 6ths, and 7ths can be major intervals.
Unisons, 4ths, 5ths, and octaves can be perfect intervals.
Major intervals can become, when altered, minor, diminished, and augmented intervals.
Perfect intervals can become, when altered, diminished and augmented intervals.

Figure 6.1:
a. C - A is a major 6th because A is the 6th note of the C major scale. For an interval to be major, the top note must be a member of the bottom notes major scale.
b. C - A♭ is a minor 6th. When the notes of a major interval are made closer together by a half step, it becomes minor.
c. C - A♭♭ is a diminished 6th. When the notes of a major interval are made closer together by a whole step (2 half steps), it becomes diminished.
d. C - A♯ is an augmented 6th. When the notes of a major interval are made further apart by a half step, it becomes augmented.

Figure 6.1

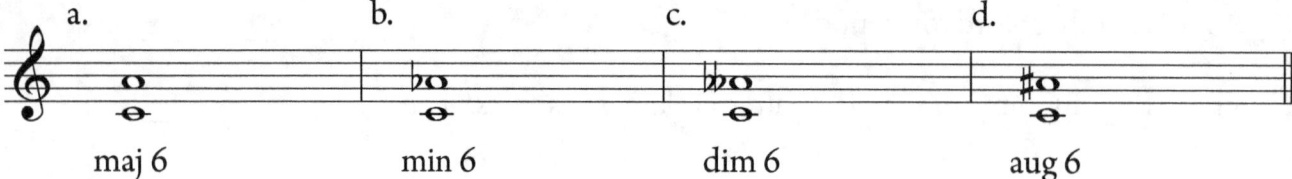

Figure 6.2:
a. C - F is a perfect 4th because F is the 4th note of the C major scale. For an interval to be perfect, the top note must be a member of the bottom notes major scale.
b. C - F♭ is a diminished 4th. When the notes of a perfect interval are made closer together by a half step, it becomes diminished. Perfect intervals (1, 4, 5, and 8) never become minor.
c. C -F♯ is an augmented 4th. When the notes of a perfect interval are made further apart by a half step, it becomes augmented.
d. C -C is a perfect unison. Even though we consider this an interval, there is no distance between the notes C and C. This is the smallest possible interval we have in Western music.
e. C - C♭ is an augmented unison. Since the notes of a perfect unison cannot get any closer, lowering one of them will make them further apart, and the interval augmented.

Figure 6.2

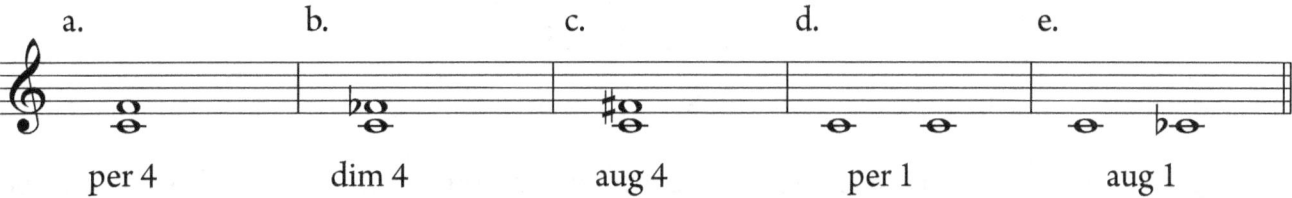

This chart shows the relationship between intervals. The arrow indicates the movement of the top note one half step.

diminished ← minor ← **major** → augmented

diminshed ← **perfect** → augmented

Any interval can be inverted or flipped upside down. When an interval is inverted the sum of the original, and the inverted interval equals nine. Study the intervals in the first measure of Figure 6.3. G -B is a major 3rd. When it is inverted it becomes B-G, a minor 6th. 3 + 6 = 9. Examine the remaining inversions.

Figure 6.3

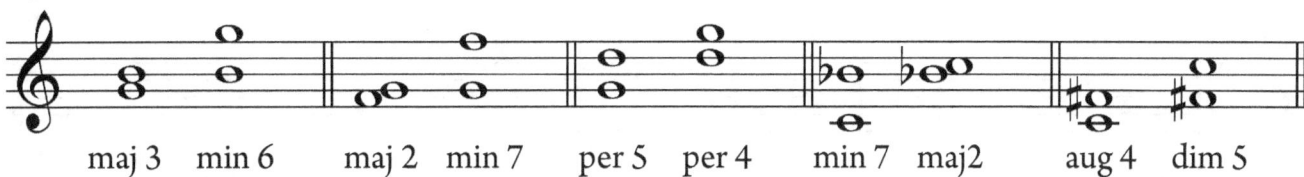

Except for perfect intervals the interval quality changes when you invert them. Here is what happens to the interval qualities when you invert them:
- major becomes minor
- minor becomes major
- diminished becomes augmented
- augmented becomes diminished
- perfect stays perfect

The inversion of the augmented octave requires special attention. An augmented octave is larger than an octave and when it is inverted the numbers do not add up to 9. Figure 6.4 shows the inversion of the augmented octave. An aug 8 becomes a dim 8 when inverted. However, since a dim 8 is smaller than an octave, it becomes and aug 1 when inverted.

Figure 6.4

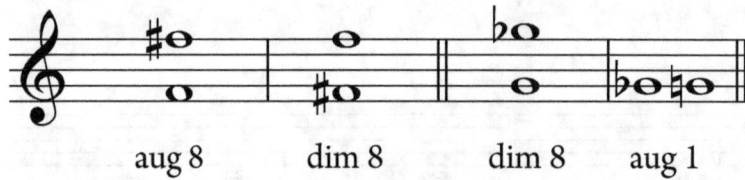

If we change one of the notes of an interval enharmonically, the number and quality will change. The intervals in each measure of Figure 6.5 sound the same but are named differently.
The top note in example a) is changed enharmonically from B♭ to A♯, and the bottom note in example b) is changed enharmonically from A♭ to G♯. Even though the pitch does not change, the interval number and quality changes.

Figure 6.5

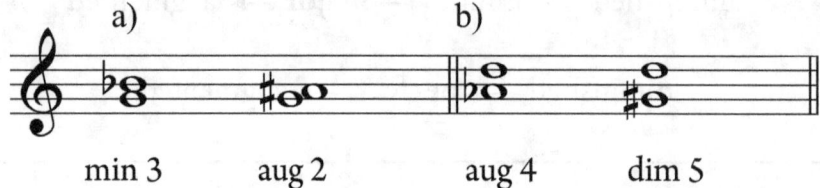

1. Name the following intervals. Change the top note enharmonically and rename them.

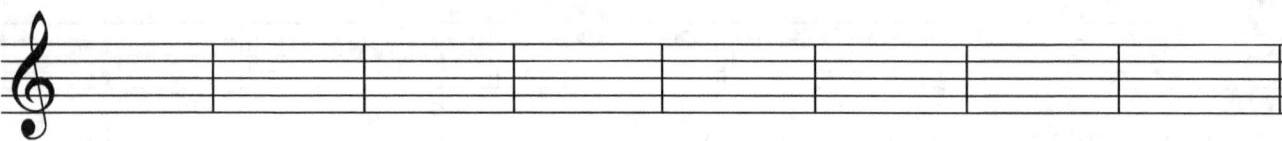

2. Name the following intervals. Invert them and rename them.

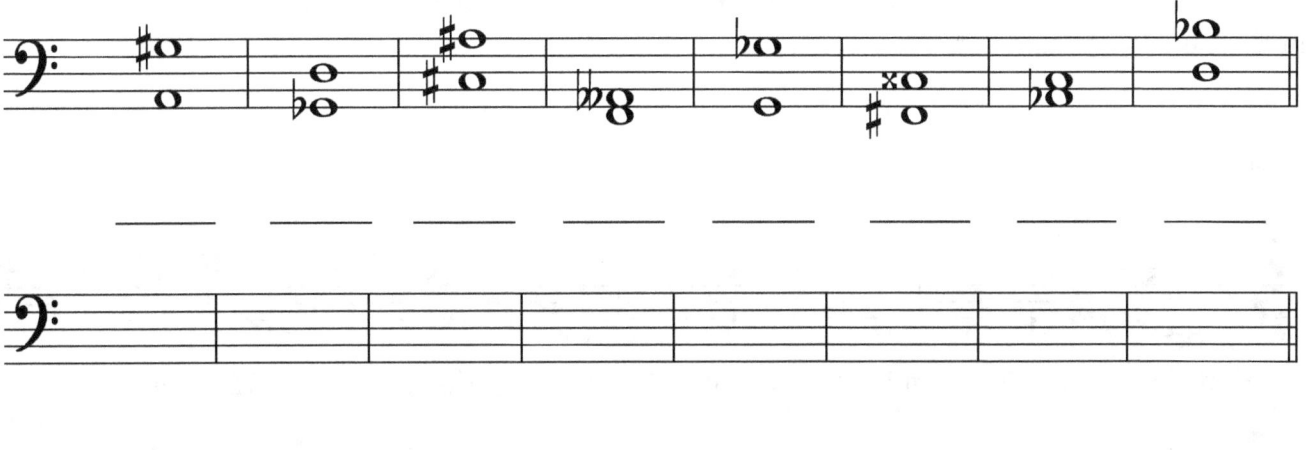

Compound Intervals

Intervals larger than an octave are called *compound intervals*.

Figure 6.6

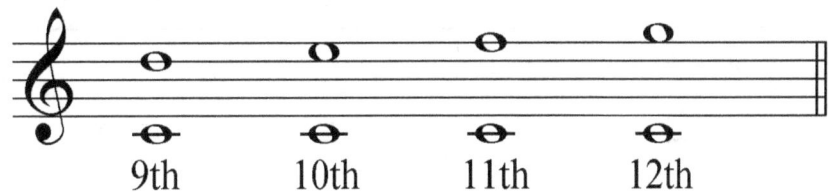

The easiest way to solve a compound interval is to bring the top note down an octave. This puts the interval in its simple form, which is an octave or less. The compound interval will be the same as the simple interval plus 7. The quality of the interval remains the same from simple to compound form.

Figure 6.7

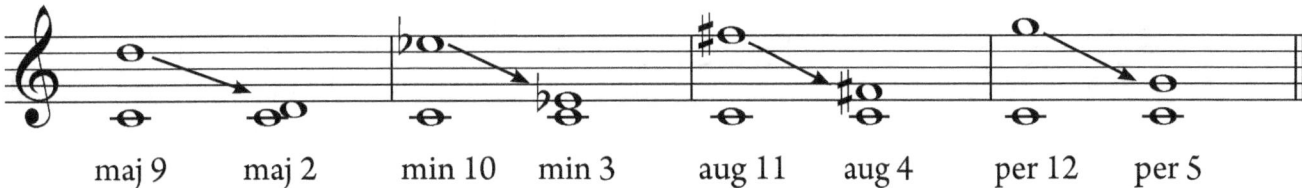

The compound interval can be inverted by moving the upper note down an octave and the lower note up an octave. This reverses the notes. See Figure 6.8. The size of the compound interval and its inversion will add up to 16.

Figure 6.8

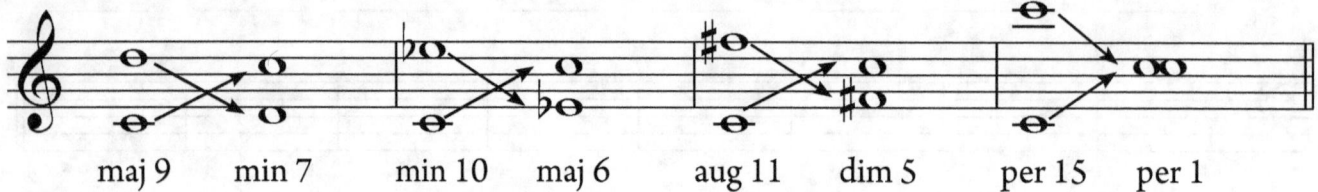

maj 9   min 7   min 10   maj 6   aug 11   dim 5   per 15   per 1

1. Name the following intervals. Invert and rename them.

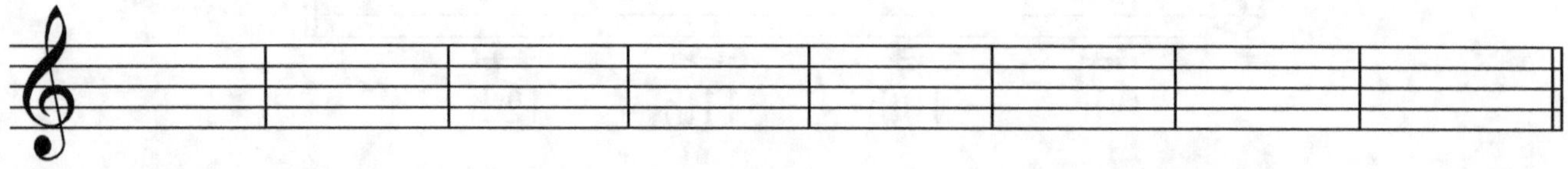

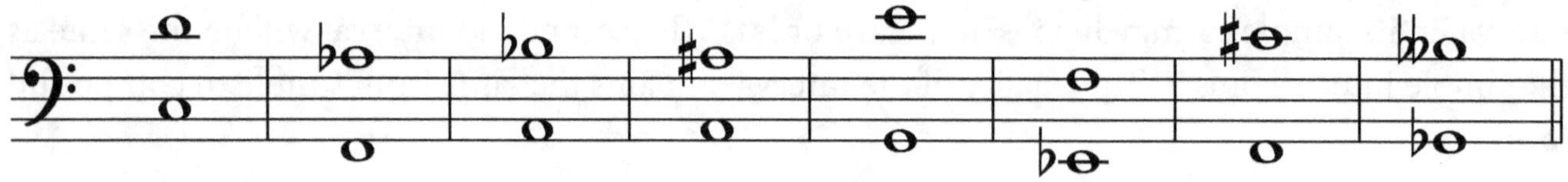

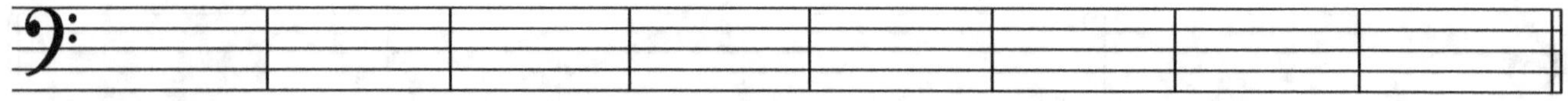

2. Write the following intervals above the given notes.

   min 10   per 11   maj 9   maj 10   dim 12   min 9   per 12   aug 11

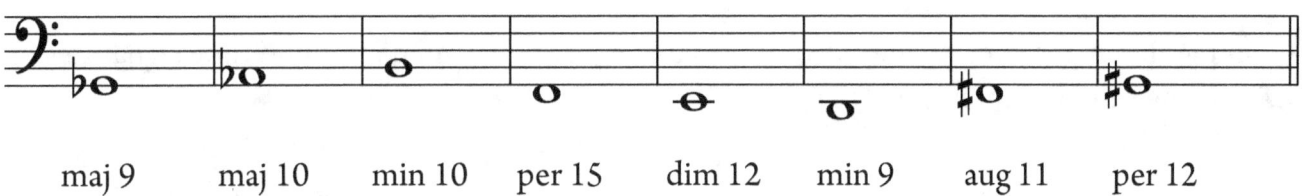

   maj 9   maj 10   min 10   per 15   dim 12   min 9   aug 11   per 12

3. Name the intervals under the brackets.

1. _____ 2. _____ 3. _____ 4. _____ 5. _____

4. Name the intervals indicated by the lines.

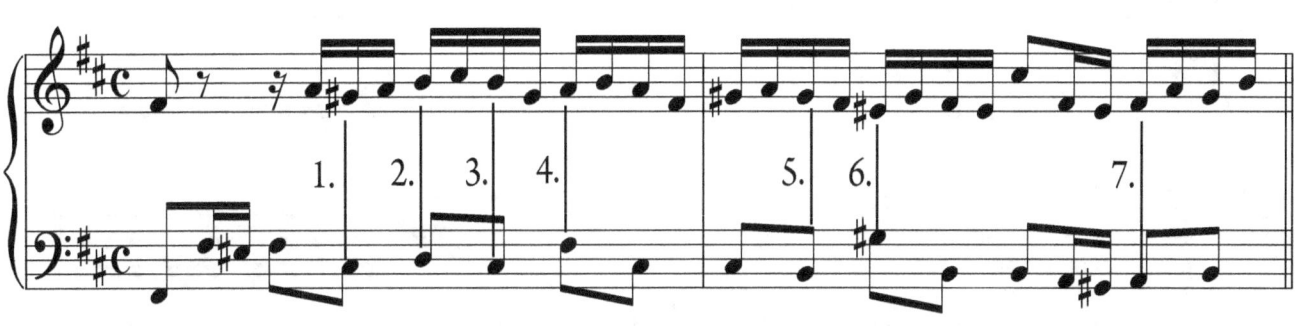

1. _____ 2. _____ 3. _____ 4. _____ 5. _____

6. _____ 7. _____

7
Time

Simple time signatures divide the beat into two equal parts and compound time signatures divide the beat into three equal parts.

1. Add barlines according to the time signatures.

Irregular Divisions of the Beat

In simple time the beat may be divided into irregular groups of three, five, six or seven. A group of 5, 6, or 7 notes is played in the time of a group of 4 of the same kind in simple time.

Figure 7.1

In compound time the beat may be divided into irregular groups of two, four, five, or seven. In compound time the main beat is a dotted note. Each group represents one beat (three pulses). Some of the groups look the same in simple and compound time. To determine the beat in the melody with irregular groupings look at the time signature and the other beats in the bar.

Figure 7.2

1. Add barlines according to the time signatures.

Rests in Simple Time

A whole rest is used to indicate one complete measure of silence for every time signature except 4/2. In 4/2 meter, the double whole or breve rest is used to indicate a complete measure of silence.

Figure 7.3

When adding rests to complete a measure of music it is important to show each beat clearly. In Figure 7.4 the first two measures contain one beat of music and are completed with one rest for the remaining beat. In the remaining two measures, each incomplete beat is finished before moving on to the next beat.

Figure 7.4

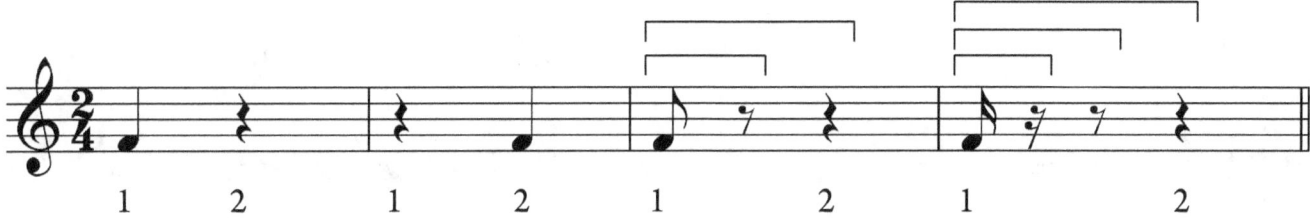

In simple triple meter never join beats two and three into one rest. Beats one and two may be joined or written as two separate rests Figure 7.5.

Figure 7.5

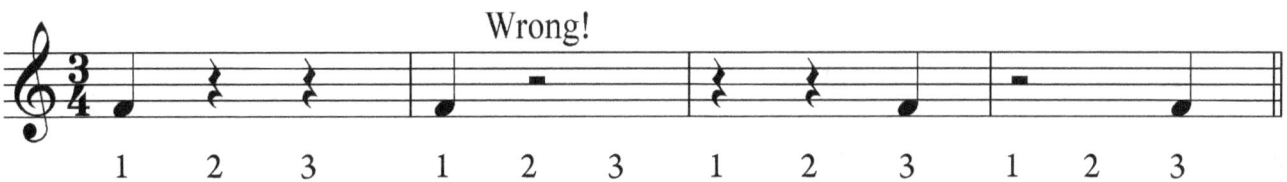

In simple quadruple meter join beats one and two into one rest and join beats three and four into one rest. Never join beats two and three into one rest Figure 7.6.

Figure 7.6

Rests in Compound Time

Dotted rests are not used in simple meter. They are used in compound meter and equal one beat. Two beats may be joined into one dotted rest to represent the first half or the last half of a measure in compound quadruple meter.

Figure 7.7

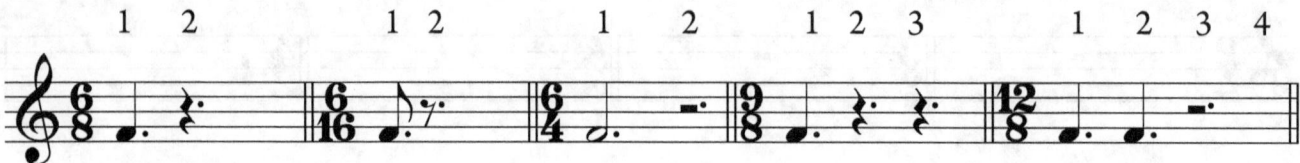

In compound meter each beat equals 3 pulses. The first 2 pulses of a beat should be joined into one rest as shown in Figure 7.8 a) and b). The last 2 pulses of a beat should use separate rests as shown in Figure 7.8 c) and d). Do not join pulses 2 and 3 into one rest.

Figure 7.8

In compound triple meter beats 1 and 2 may be joined into one rest. Do not join beats 2 and 3 into one rest.

Figure 7.9

In compound quadruple time beats 1 and 2 should be joined into one rest. Beats 3 and 4 should be joined into one rest. Do not join beats 2 and 3 into one rest.

Figure 7.10

1. Add rests under the brackets to complete the following measures.

Hybrid Meters

Hybrid meters are a combination of simple and compound time. Each measure is made up of dotted (groups of three) and non-dotted (groups of two) notes. Because of this, some beats are longer than others. The top number of a hybrid time signature shows the number of pulses in a measure and the bottom number shows which note gets the pulse.

Hybrid Duple Time

In *hybrid duple time,* the top number of the time signature is always 5. The bottom number may be 4, 8, or 16. There are two beats and five pulses in each measure. This consists of one beat that is worth three pulses and one beat that is worth two pulses. The beats may be grouped as 3 +2 or 2 + 3 as shown in Figure 7.11.

Figure 7.11

Hybrid Triple Time

In *hybrid triple time,* the top number of the time signature may be 7 or 8. The bottom number may be 4, 8, or 16. In Figure 7.12 there are three beats and seven pulses in each measure. This consists of one beat that is worth three pulses and two beats that are worth two pulses each. The beats may be grouped as 3 +2 +2, 2 + 3 + 2 or 2 + 2 + 3.

Figure 7.12

In Figure 7.13 there are three beats and eight pulses in each measure. There are two compound beats and one simple beat. This consists of two beats that are worth three pulses and one beat that is worth two pulses each. The beats may be grouped as 3 +3 +2, 2 + 3 + 3 or 3 + 2 + 3. Do not confuse this with 4/4 which also has 8 eighth notes. 4/4 is grouped into four groups of two eighth notes.

Figure 7.13

Hybrid Quadruple Time

In *hybrid quadruple time,* the top number of the time signature may be 9, 10, or 11. The bottom number may be 4, 8, or 16. There are four beats in each measure. This hybrid meter is less common than the other two. Figure 7.14 shows some of the possibilities for hybrid quadruple time, but many groupings are possible. The following is the beat breakdown for these time signatures:

- One dotted beat and three non-dotted beats equaling 4 beats and 9 pulses.(7.14a.)
- Two dotted beats and two non-dotted beats equaling 4 beats and 10 pulses.(7.14b.)
- Three dotted beats and one non-dotted beat equaling 4 beats and 11pulses.(7.14c.)

The arrangement of the beats in each time signature can vary.

Figure 7.14

1. Add bar lines according to the time signatures.

2. Add time signatures to the following two measure examples.

3. Add bar lines according to the time signatures.

- *In hybrid time a whole rest indicates a full measure of silence. as shown in* Figure 7.15.

Figure 7.15

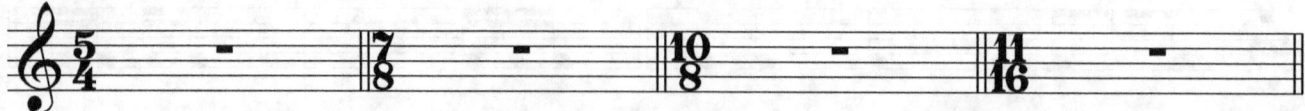

- *When adding rests in hybrid time, show each each beat with one rest when possible.*

In Figure 7.16 there are two beats in each bar. Each beat is indicated with one rest. Measure a) completes the second beat with a quarter rest indicating one beat. Measure b) needs a dotted quarter to complete the first beat. In each measure you can clearly see one 3 pulse beat and one 2 pulse beat.

Figure 7.16

- *If a measure has incomplete beats, finish them before moving on to the rest of the measure.*

In Figure 7.17 a) the first beat is completed with a sixteenth rest and two eighth rests. Do not join pulse two and three into one rest.

- *Use dotted rests to show one complete compound beat.*

Figure 7.17 b) is another option for rest placement. Here, the first beat is treated as the simple beat and the second, compound beat is shown as a dotted rest. Both measures are correct.

- *Combine the first two beats into one rest in hydrid triple. Combine the first two beats and last beats into one rest in quadruple time.*

In Figure 7.17 c) the first two beats of 7/8 are joined into one rest. The last two beats of 11/16 are joined into one rest.
There are many correct ways to complete these bars with rests. It depends where the simple and compound beats occur within the measure.

Figure 7.17

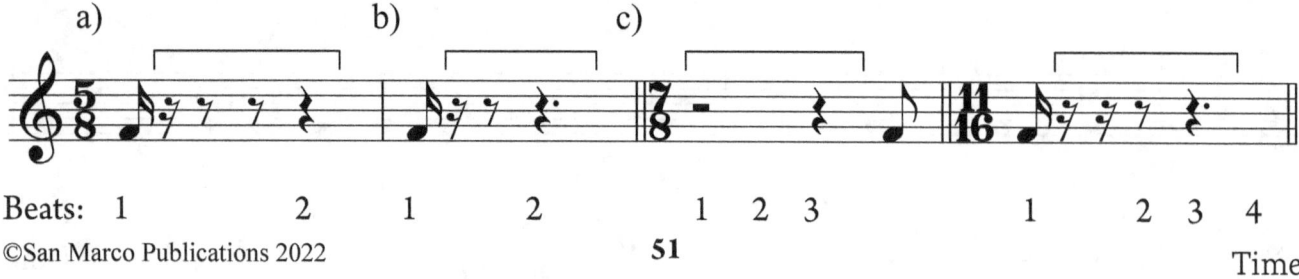

The examples in Figure 7.18 show incorrect and correct rest groupings in a measure. This should help you avoid some common errors when writing rests in hydrid time.

Figure 7.18

1. Add rests complete the following measures.

8
Triads

Review

The three notes of a triad are known as the root, third and fifth. The quality of a triad is determined by the intervals formed between the root and third and the root and fifth.

Figure 8.1 shows the four different triad qualities. Note the root/quality chord symbols.

Figure 8.1

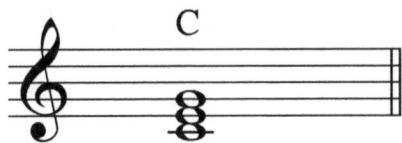

A ***major triad*** consist of the intervals of a major 3rd and a perfect 5th above the root.

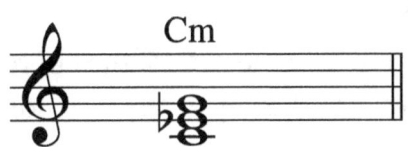

A ***minor triad*** consist of the intervals of a minor 3rd and a perfect 5th above the root.

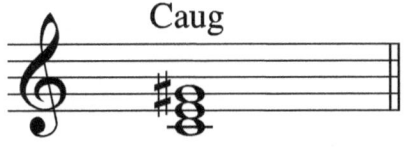

An ***augmented triad*** consist of the intervals of a major 3rd and an augmented 5th above the root.

A ***diminished triad*** consist of the intervals of a minor 3rd and a diminished 5th above the root.

Chord Symbols

Functional Chord Symbols

Functional chord symbols are Roman numerals that are placed under the staff. They identify the root of the chord by the scale degree on which it is built. This symbol also indicates a chords function. For example, V is a dominant function chord, and I is a tonic function chord.

An uppercase Roman numeral indicates a major triad (**I, V**)
A lowercase Roman numeral indicates a minor triad (**ii, iv**)
An uppercase Roman numeral with the plus + sign indicates an augmented triad (**III⁺**)
A lowercase Roman numeral with a degree ° sign indicates a diminished triad. (**vii°**)

Figure 8.2

Root/Quality Chord Symbols

Root/quality chord symbols are letters placed above the staff. They identify the root of the chord by its letter name and state the quality of the chord. They do not indicate the key or the function of the chord within the key.

An uppercase letter indicates a major triad (**D, F, B♭**)
An uppercase letter with an 'm' indicates a minor triad (**Dm, Fm**)
An uppercase letter with 'aug' indicates an augmented triad (**Caug**)
A uppercase letter with 'dim' indicates a diminished triad. (**C♯dim**) or (**C♯°**)

Figure 8.3

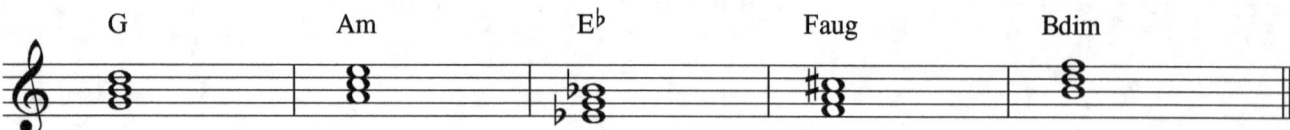

Triads Built on Major and Minor Scales

Figure 8.4 contains all of the triads built on the major scale. Major triads occur on $\hat{1}$, $\hat{4}$, and $\hat{5}$. Minor triads occur on $\hat{2}$, $\hat{3}$, and $\hat{6}$. A diminished triad occurs on $\hat{7}$.

Figure 8.4
Major scale

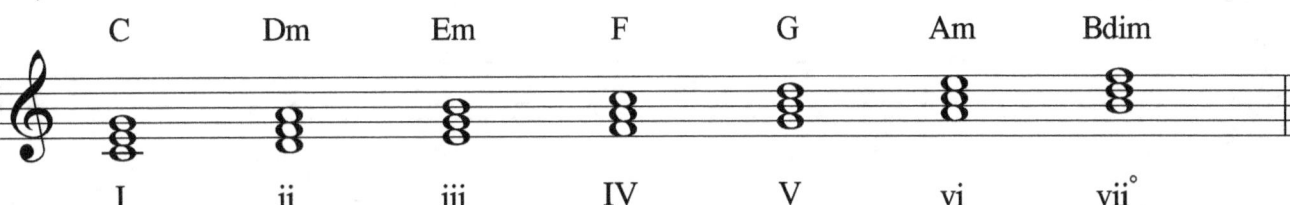

Figure 8.5 contains all of the triads built on the natural minor scale. Major triads occur on $\hat{3}$, $\hat{6}$, and $\hat{7}$. Minor triads occur on $\hat{1}$, $\hat{4}$, and $\hat{5}$. A diminished triad occurs on $\hat{2}$.

Figure 8.5
Natural minor scale

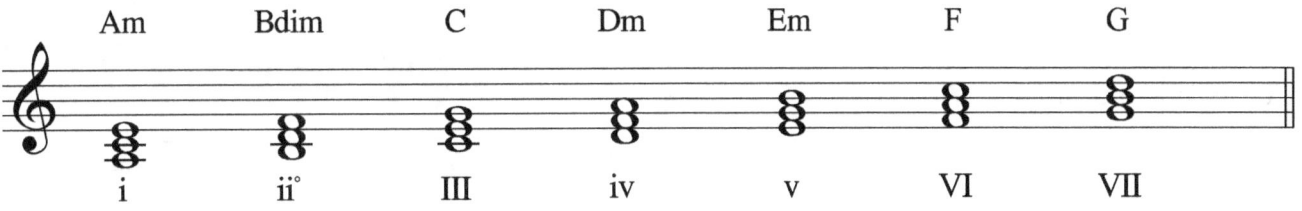

Figure 8.6 contains all of the triads built on the harmonic minor scale. Major triads occur on $\hat{5}$ and $\hat{6}$. Minor triads occur on $\hat{1}$ and $\hat{4}$. Diminished triads occur on $\hat{2}$ and $\hat{7}$. An augmented triad occurs on $\hat{3}$.

Figure 8.6
Harmonic minor scale

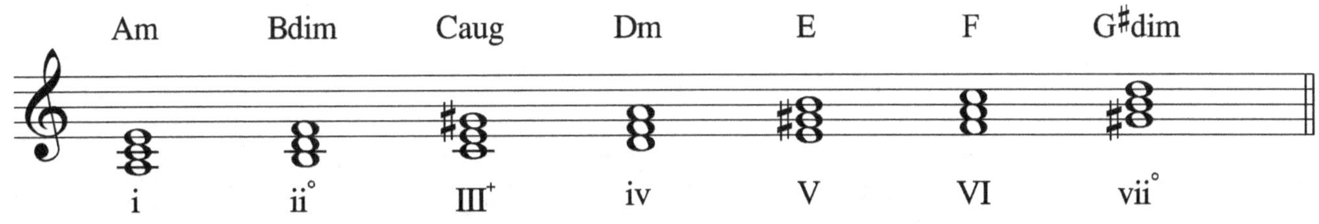

1. Write triads on the following scales. Add the functional and root/quality chords symbols.

G major

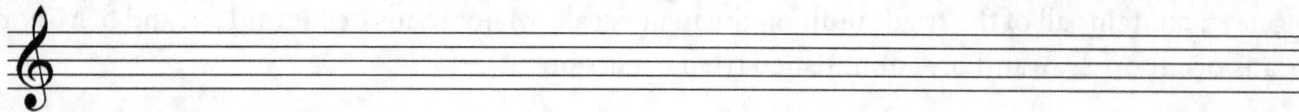

D harmonic minor

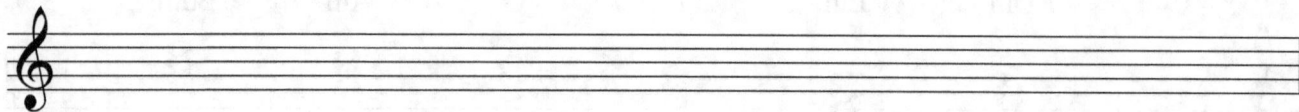

C# natural minor

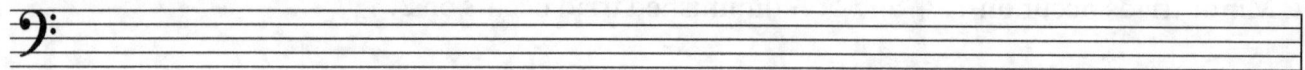

F harmonic minor

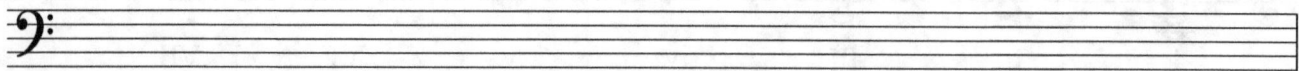

2. For the following triads: 1. Name the **major** key. 2. Write the functional and root/quality chord symbols for each. The first one is done for you.

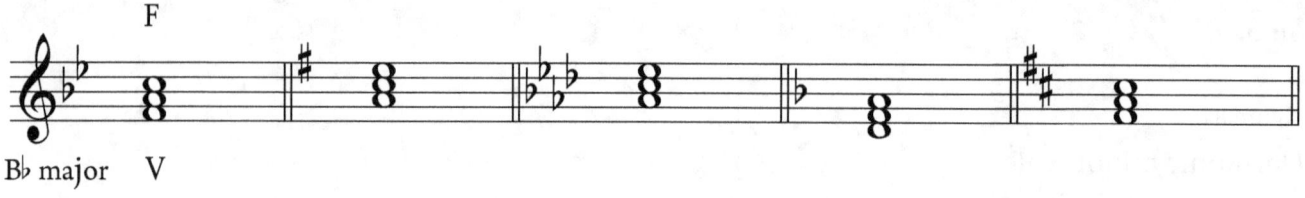

Bb major   V

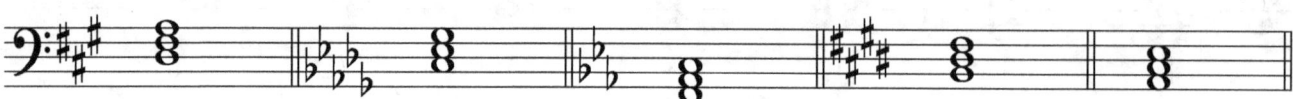

3. Write the following triads using a key signature for each. Add the functional and root/quality chord symbols.

i. The tonic triad of B major
ii. The mediant triad of G harmonic minor
iii. The supertonic triad of E natural minor
iv. The leading tone triad of B harmonic minor
v. The dominant triad of C harmonic minor

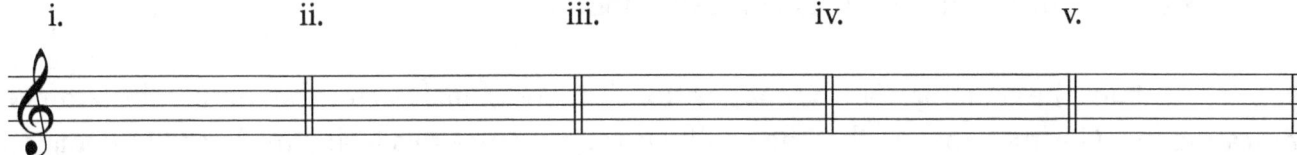

4. For the following chords: 1. Name the **harmonic minor** key. 2. Write the functional and root/quality chord symbols for each. The first one is done for you.

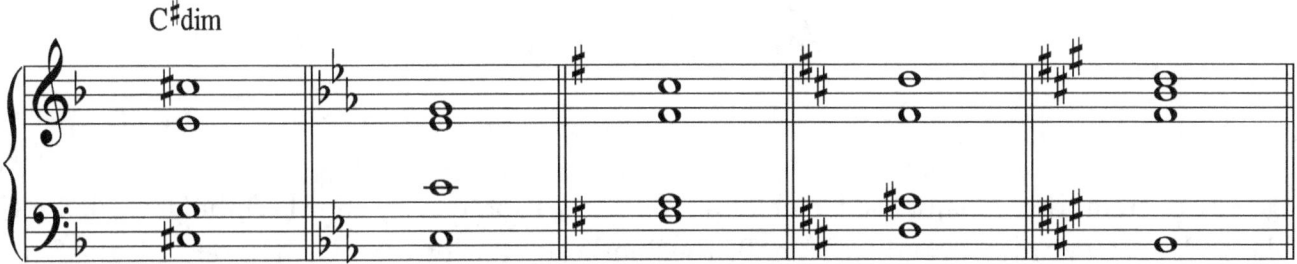

D minor   vii°

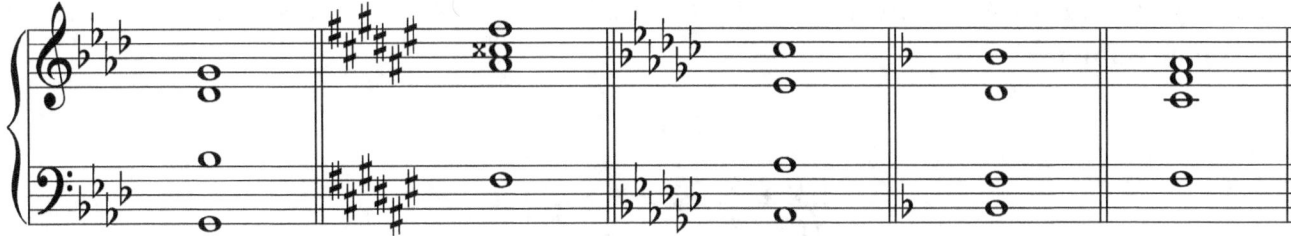

Triad Inversions

Triads may appear in root position and two *inversions*. ***Root position triads*** have the root as the lowest note. ***First inversion triads*** have the 3rd as the lowest note. ***Second inversion triads*** have the 5th as the lowest note.

Inverted chords help to make music more interesting. Inversions can create smoother motion between chords. They are used to make a bass line fluid and musical. This type of movement is called ***voice leading***. Using root position chords all the time can create a disjunct, uneven bass line that jumps around too much. Inversions can make it smoother.

Figure 8.7 contains the G major triad in root position. The root/quality chord symbol is the letter G, indicating that G is the root and that the quality is major. Since this is the tonic triad in G major, the functional chord symbol is the Roman numeral I. Triads in root position use the Roman numeral alone.

Figure 8.7

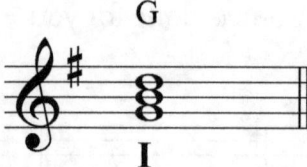

Figure 8.8 contains the G major triad in first inversion. The root/quality chord symbol is the letter G followed by a forward slash and the letter B. The B indicates the lowest note of the chord. The functional chord symbol is I^6. The '6' comes from the interval between the lowest note B and the G.

Figure 8.8

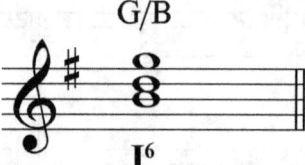

Figure 8.9 contains the G major triad in second inversion. The root/quality chord symbol is the letter G followed by a forward slash and the letter D. The D indicates the lowest note of the chord. The functional chord symbol is I^6_4. The $^6_4$ comes from the intervals between the lowest note and the upper notes. D to B is a 6th and D to G is a 4th. Second inversion triads always use $^6_4$ next to the Roman numeral.

Figure 8.9

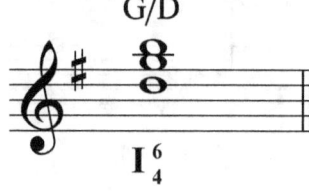

Figure 8.10 illustrates the chord symbols for the C minor triad in root position and inversions. In root/quality chord symbols, minor triads are indicated with an "m" beside the uppercase letter. In functional chord symbols, minor triads are shown with a lower case Roman numeral.

figure 8.10

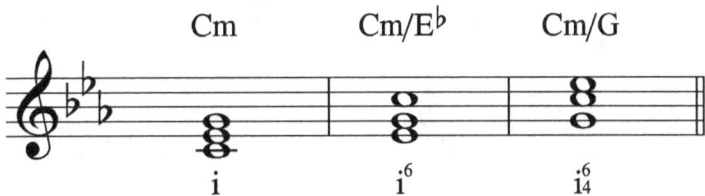

1. The following triads are in major keys. Name the key and write the root/quality and functional chord symbols for each. The first one is done for you.

2. The following triads are in harmonic minor keys. Name the key and write the root/quality and functional chord symbols for each. The first one is done for you.

©San Marco Publications 2022

3. Name the key and add functional and root/quality chord symbols to the following chord progressons.

Key:____

Key:____

9
Seventh Chords

Review - The Dominant 7th Chord

A triad is a three note chord. Chords in Western music are built on 3rds. When we built triads on the notes of the major and minor scales, we stacked two 3rds onto the root. If we place another 3rd on top of a triad, we get a 7th chord. These chords are named '7th' because the last note added is seven notes away from the root.

One of the most common seventh chords is the **dominant seventh**. The functional chord symbol for the dominant seventh is V^7. This means that the chord is built on scale degree $\hat{5}$ (the dominant) and there is the interval of a seventh above the root of the chord. This chord contains four notes, the root, 3rd, 5th, and 7th. V^7 is a major triad with a minor 7th above the root. In other words, the intervals above the root are a major 3rd, a perfect 5th, and a minor 7th. The dominant 7th is the same in tonic major and minor keys (e.g., G major and G minor have the same V^7 - DF#AC).

When writing the functional chord symbols for inversions of V^7, some of the numbers are omitted. Figure 9.1 shows the numbers that indicate the intervals that occur above the lowest note of the dominant 7th. Figure 9.2 shows the actual functional chord symbols used for V^7 and its inversions.

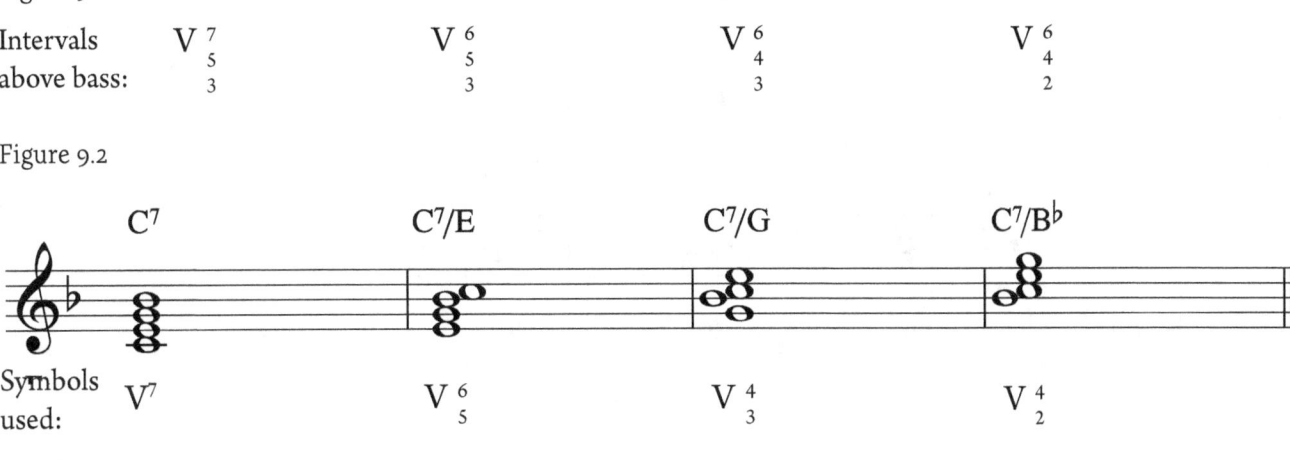

1. Name the key and write the functional and root/quality chord symbols for the following dominant 7th chords.

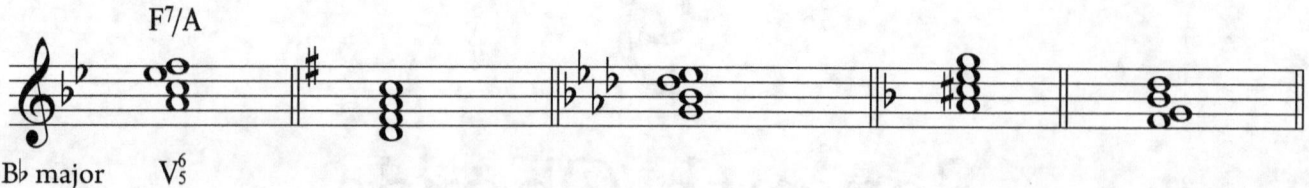

B♭ major V^6_5 F^7/A

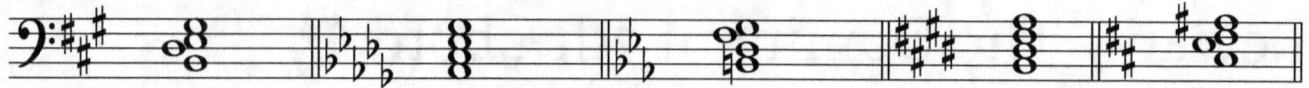

The Diminished Seventh Chord

The ***diminished seventh*** is built on raised $\hat{7}$ in the minor key. Figure 9.3 shows the diminished seventh chord built on raised $\hat{7}$ in A minor. The functional chord symbol is vii^{o7}.

Figure 9.3

A minor   vii^{o7}

Figure 9.4 shows that this chord consists of a diminished triad with a diminished 7th above the root of the chord. The root/quality symbol is G♯dim^7 or G♯^{o7}.

Figure 9.4

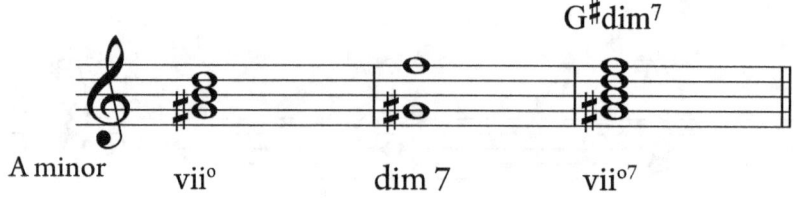

A minor   vii^o dim 7   vii^{o7} G♯dim^7

©San Marco Publications 2022   Seventh Chords

1. Write the following diminished 7th chords using key signatures.

G minor	F minor	E minor	D minor	C# minor
vii°7	vii°7	vii°7	vii°7	vii°7

2. For the following chords name the: 1. Root 2. Quality 3. Position

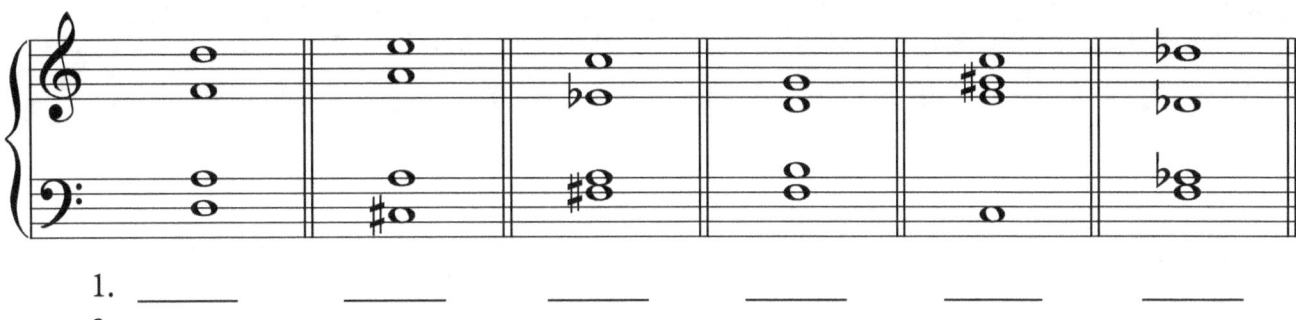

1. _____   _____   _____   _____   _____   _____
2. _____   _____   _____   _____   _____   _____
3. _____   _____   _____   _____   _____   _____

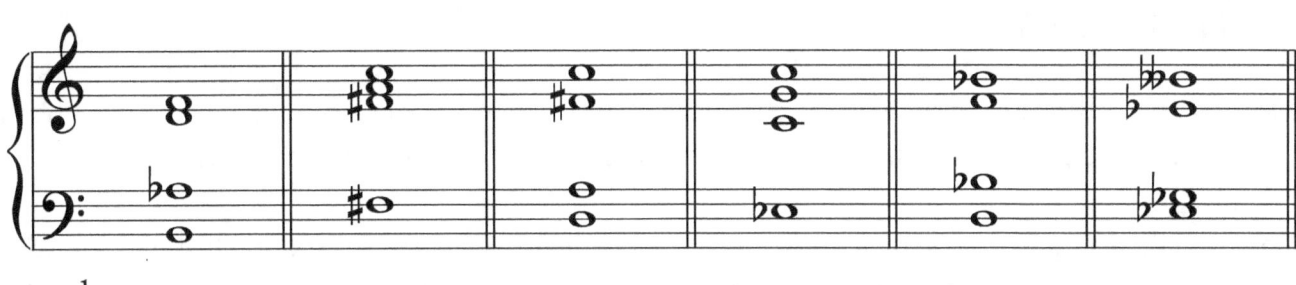

1. _____   _____   _____   _____   _____   _____
2. _____   _____   _____   _____   _____   _____
3. _____   _____   _____   _____   _____   _____

1. _____   _____   _____   _____   _____   _____
2. _____   _____   _____   _____   _____   _____
3. _____   _____   _____   _____   _____   _____

3. Write the following chords using accidentals.

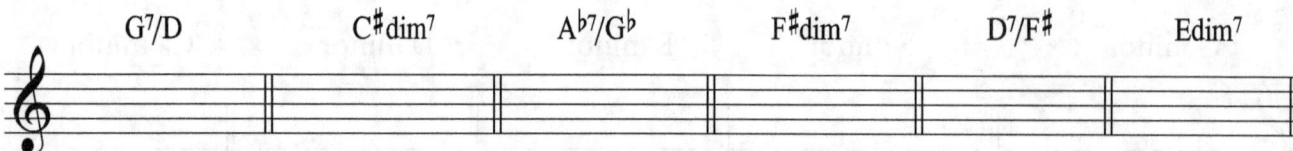

4. Write the following chords according to the functional chord symbols.

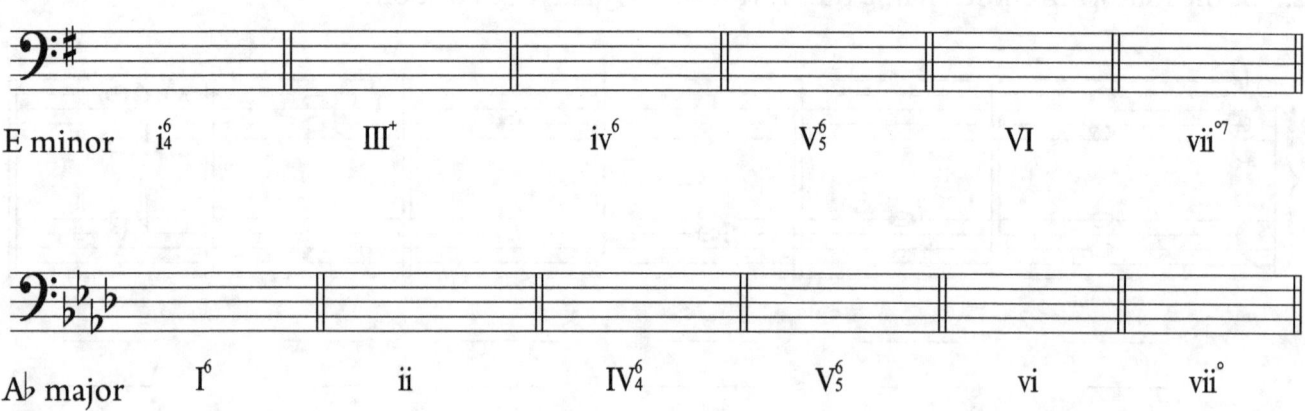

Other Chords

Composers of the late 19th, 20th, and 21st centuries expanded harmonic language and chord structure. The following chords added variety, interest, and dissonant tension to their works.

Chords called ***tone clusters***, or ***cluster chords*** are shown in Figure 9.5. A tone cluster is a chord made up of at least three consecutive tones in a scale. Sometimes they are based on the chromatic scale and are separated by half steps. For example, three adjacent piano keys (such as F, F♯, and G) played simultaneously produce a tone cluster. Tone clusters may also be made up of adjacent diatonic tones. The first clusters were written for the piano, but soon they were being used in music for other mediums. Some modern composers use large keyboard tone clusters called ***forearm clusters***. These are performed by slamming the forearm onto the keys. Examples c) and d) show different ways that forearm clusters can be notated.

Figure 9.5

Polychords are formed by combining two or more different chords. Only triads and 7th chords are combined to form polychords. Most polychords combine elements of two different keys or modes. Figure 9.6 shows how Ravel used two different chords at the same time to produce a polychord. Here, the right plays a G major triad, and the left hand plays a D♯ minor 7th chord.

Figure 9.6

Maurice Ravel
Piano Concerto in G (1931)

Quartal chords are chords made up of a series of fourths. This is in contrast to more familiar chords (like major, minor, dominant, diminished, augmented) that are built on thirds, (tertian chords). Composers sometimes use these chords in intermittant or brief passages in a composition for their unique effect. Figure 9.7 contains a famous quartal chord used by the composer Alexander Scriabin (1871 - 1915). This chord is known as the *mystic chord*. Scriabin based some of his later works on this quartal chord including his Sonata No. 5, Op. 53. In jazz music quartal chords were made popular by McCoy Tyner (John Coltrane's piano player). They have a jazzy sound and work well in modal music.

Figure 9.7

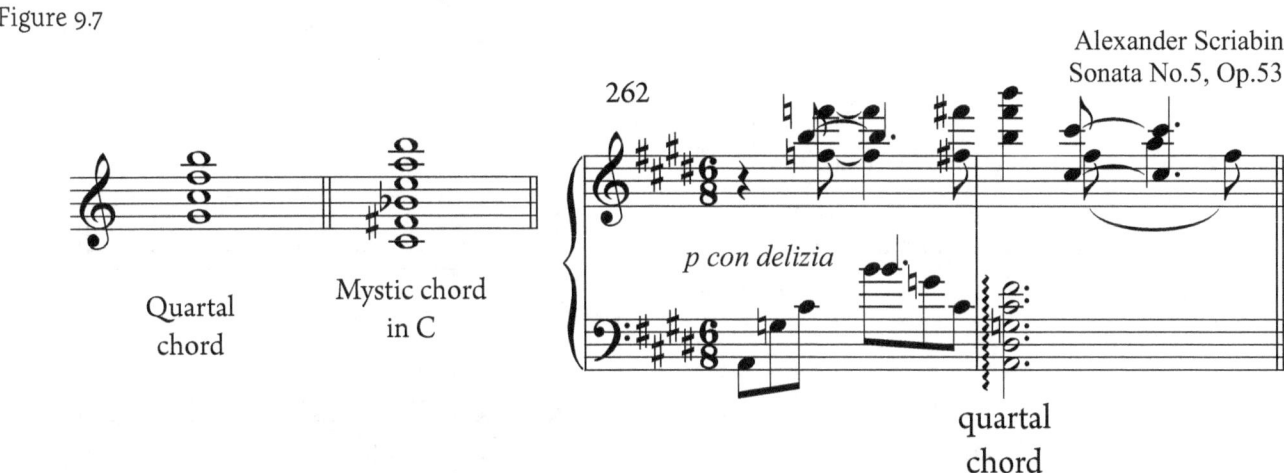

Alexander Scriabin
Sonata No.5, Op.53

1. Match each chord with its description.

_____ a tone cluster or cluster chord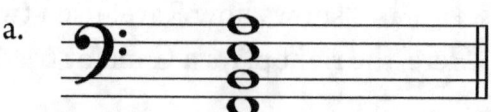

_____ vii°7 of A harmonic minor

_____ a quartal chord

_____ V7 of E minor

_____ a polychord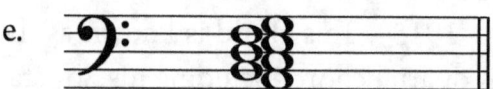

_____ V4/2 of G major

_____ C augmented triad in 1st inversion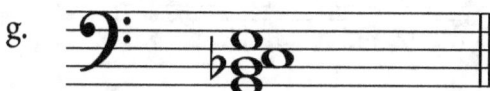

_____ V4/3 of F major

10
Cadences

Review - The Authentic Cadence

The most frequently used final cadence is the ***authentic cadence***. It is the strongest and most conclusive cadence. It consists of the chords V - I or V - i (in minor keys). An authentic cadence that ends with the tonic as the top note of the I chord is considered a ***perfect authentic cadence***. This reflects its degree of finality. Figure 10.1 contains two perfect authentic cadences in keyboard style.

Figure 10.1

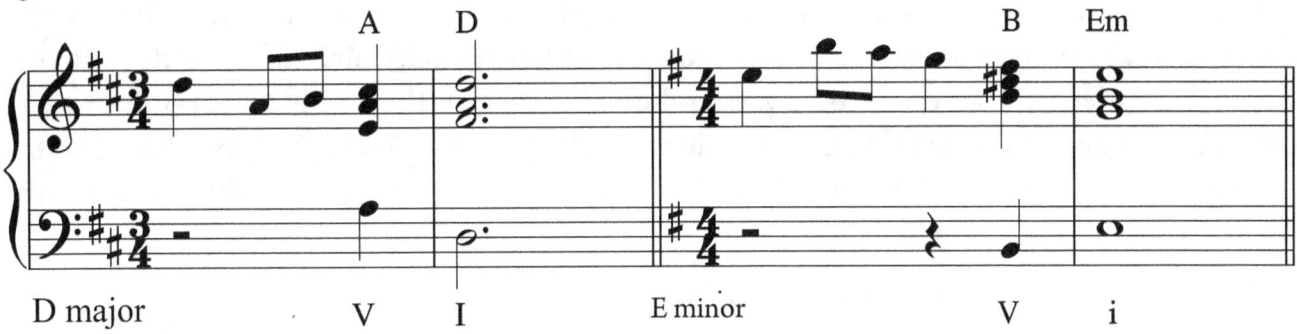

The cadences in Figure 10.2 are considered ***imperfect authentic cadences*** because they end on a note other than the tonic. The D major cadence ends with the 5th (A) as the final and top note. The E minor cadence ends on the 3rd (G) as the final and top note. These are still final cadences but do not sound as strong and final as a perfect authentic cadence which ends with tonic as the final and top note.

Figure 10.2

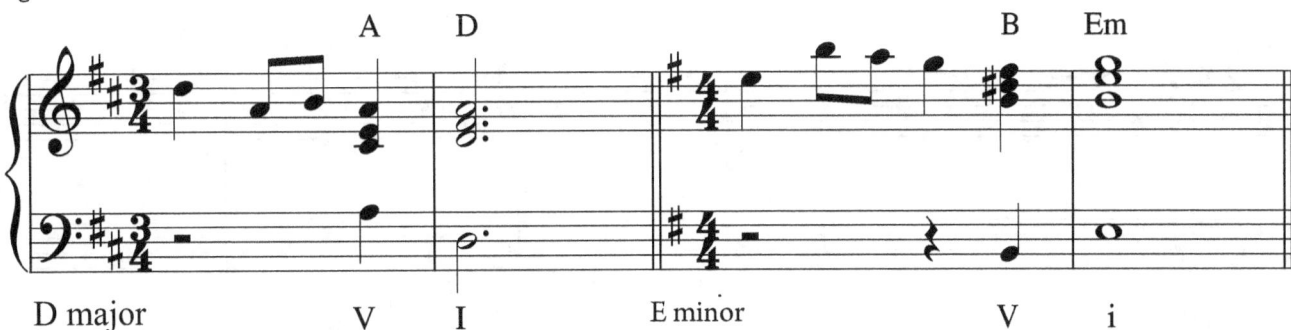

V^7 - I is also an authentic cadence. Figure 10.3 shows two authentic cadences using V^7. In the first example in G major, the V^7 chord is complete using all four notes, D F♯ A C. In the D minor example the V^7 chord is considered incomplete. Here, the root is doubled, and the 5th of the chord is left out, A C♯ G A. Both of these examples are correct. The root of each chord must always be in the bass.

Figure 10.3

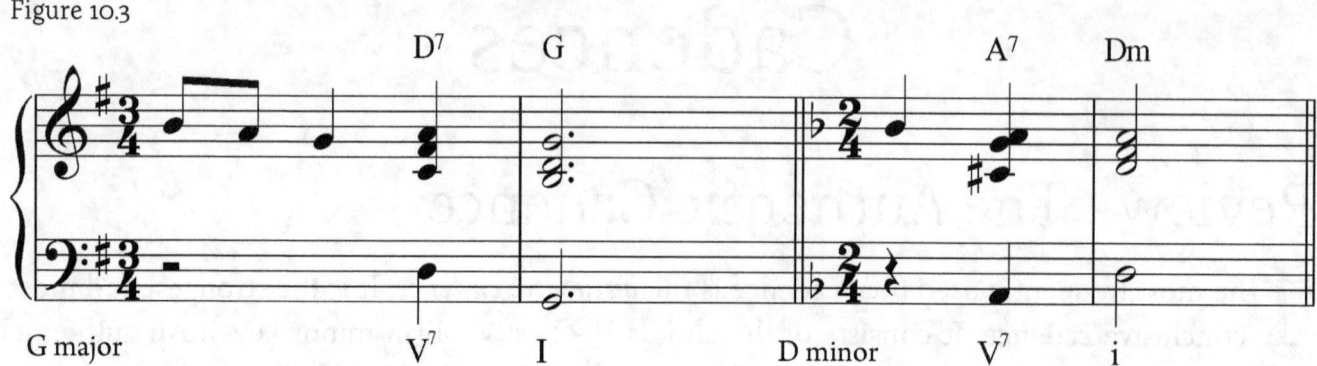

The Half Cadence

The *half cadence* is a non-final cadence. It ends with the V chord. Ending a phrase on the V chord leaves the music with an open or unfinished sound. For this reason, a piece of music does not end with a half cadence. Half cadences always end on V and never the dominant seventh, since V^7 contains too many strong tones that do not allow a feeling of rest. We will study two half cadences that are shown in Figure 10.4. For the cadence IV - V, the bass rises a step and the three upper voices fall to the nearest chord tones.

Figure 10.4

©San Marco Publications 2022

1. For the following cadences: Name the key, write the functional and root/quality chord symbols and name them as half, perfect authentic, or imperfect authentic.

The Plagal Cadence

The *plagal cadence* is a final cadence. In major keys it is IV - I. In minor keys it is iv - i. Like most cadences, it moves from IV on a weak beat to I on a strong beat. Since this cadence does not contain the leading tone, it is not as final sounding as the authentic cadence. The plagal cadence is often heard at the end of church hymns harmonizing the word "Amen." This cadence has its origins in church music but is heard today in music from country to rock.

Figure 10.5 contains plagal cadences in major and minor keys.

Figure 10.5

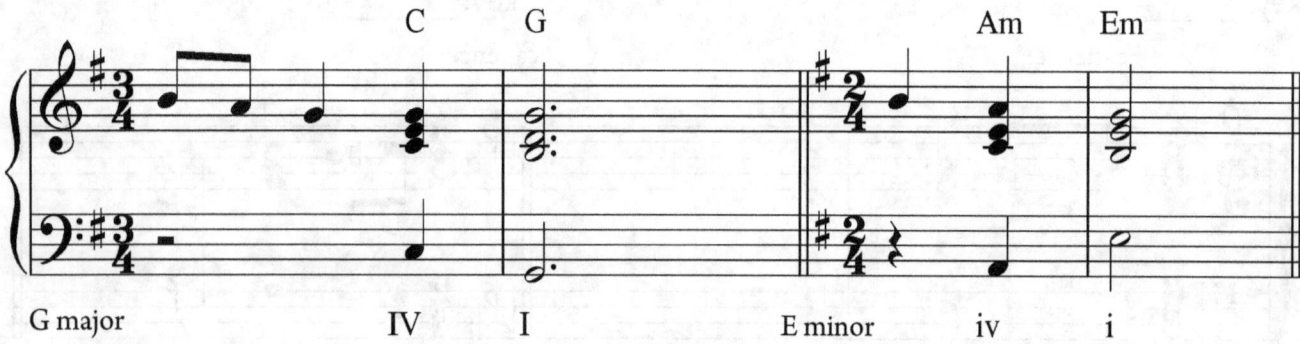

1. For the following cadences: Name the key, write the functional and root/quality chord symbols and name them as plagal, perfect authentic, imperfect authentic or half.

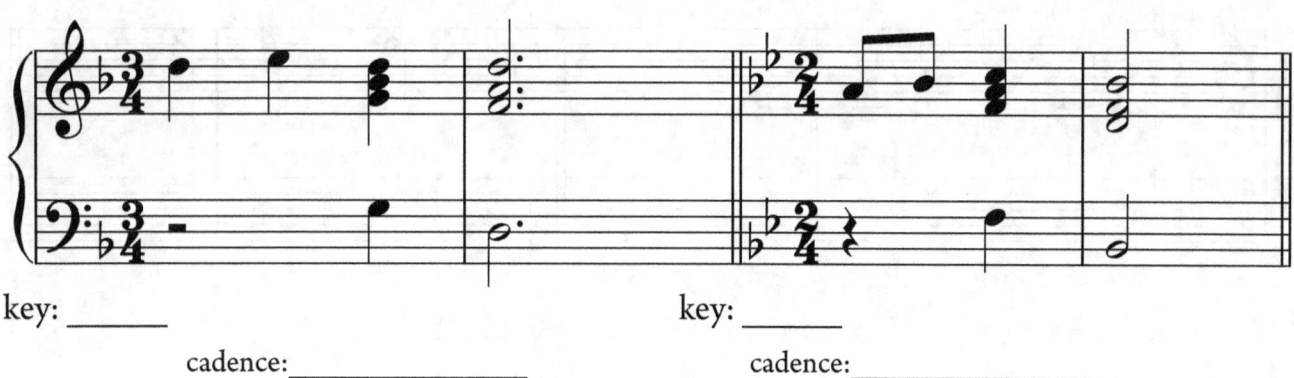

key: _____   key: _____
    cadence:_____   cadence:_____

key: _____   key: _____
    cadence:_____   cadence:_____

Writing The Plagal Cadence

Certain guidelines should be followed when writing a plagal cadence. Study the following steps for writing an plagal cadence in F major.

1. Add the key signature and rests at the beginning of the first measure. Cadences often occur over the bar line with the second chord of the cadence on a stronger beat than the first. The first chord occurs in the second half or second part of the first measure on a weaker beat. In Figure 10.6 the key signature of F major is B flat. It is placed *before* the time signature. Roman numerals indicating the functional chord symbols of the plagal cadence are placed under the staff (IV - I). Since this is 2/4 time a quarter rest is used at the beginning of the measure and the IV chord will be placed on beat 2 of the first measure. There are other options that could be used rhythmically, but this is effective. Write the bass notes for the IV and I chord in F major.

Figure 10.6

2. Write the notes of the IV chord in close position on the treble staff. Close position occurs when the notes of the triad are as close together as possible. In F major IV is B♭-D-F. These notes can be in any order as long as they stay in close position. Figure 10.7 uses quarter notes on beat 2 of the first measure for this chord.

Figure 10.7

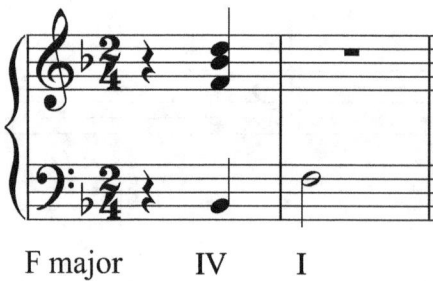

3. Write the notes of the I chord in the second measure. I in F major is F-A-C. Keep these notes as close as possible to the notes of the IV chord. In Figure 10.8 there is one note that is common to both chords (F). This F is kept in the same place in both chords (here it is the bottom note). This note is called the ***common tone***. Repeating the common tone in the same place creates smooth movement. This movement of notes from chord to chord is called ***voice leading***.

Figure 10.8

The common tone is repeated in the same place.

F major   IV   I

1. Add key signatures and write plagal cadences in keyboard style in the following keys. Write the functional chord symbols for each cadence.

A major   C minor   D major

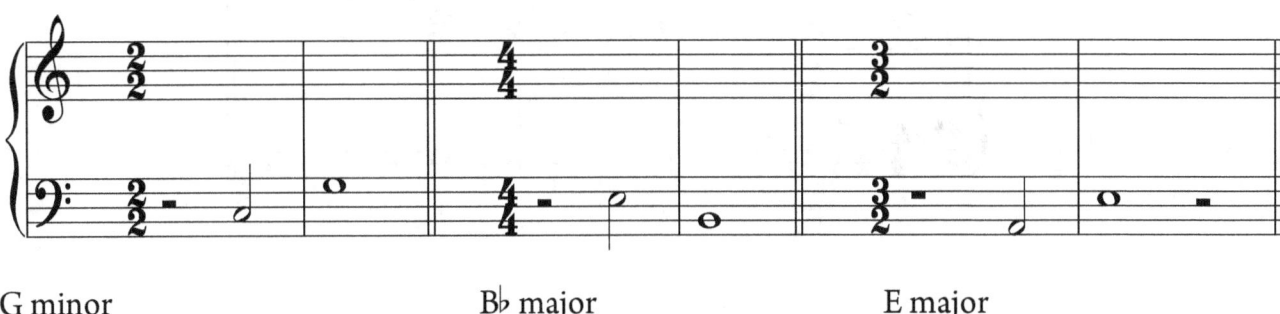

G minor   B♭ major   E major

Voice Leading

Voice leading was mentioned earlier in relation to writing cadences. Voice leading can be defined in a couple of ways.

1. It can be defined as the way we connect chords, preferably, in the smoothest possible way.
2. It can also be defined as a specific set of rules for how individual voices move from chord to chord. This is most common in four-part writing.

Figure 10.9 contains a chord progression in keyboard style. This progression is clumsy and jumps from one chord to the next.

Figure 10.9

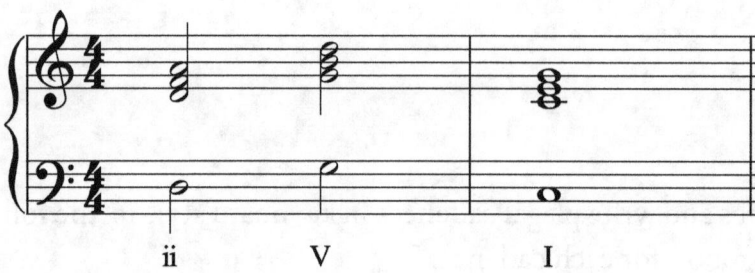

Figure 10.10 contains a much smoother version of the same chord progression. When writing chord progressions, it is best to move to the closest note of the next chord. This progression not only sounds better, but it is easier to play. These chords have common tones that are repeated in the same place between chords. This creates smoother voice leading and a better progression.

Figure 10.10

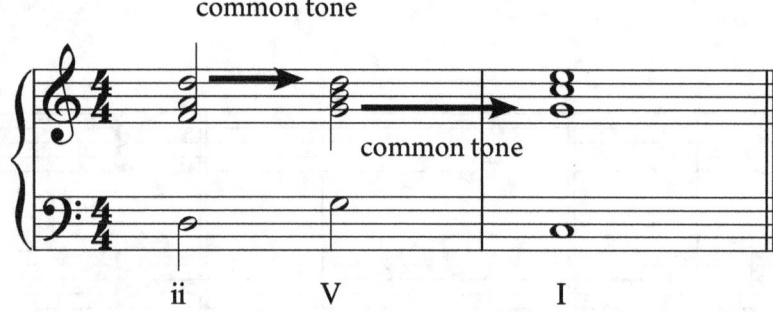

Cadences in Chorale or Four-Part Style

When cadences are written in *chorale* or *four-part style,* the chords are written in four parts. These four parts make up the four voices of a choir. The four voices are the:

Soprano, Alto, Tenor, and **Bass**

In chorale style, the soprano and alto are written on the treble staff and the tenor and bass are written on the bass staff. Figure 10.11 shows the C major chord written in different positions in chorale style. Note the following:

- The music is written on the grand staff.
- The stems of the soprano and tenor go up.
- The stems of the alto and bass go down.
- The root of each chord is doubled (written twice).
- The space between the soprano and alto and between the alto and tenor cannot exceed one octave. The space between the tenor and bass can be larger than an octave as long as it stays within each voice range.

Figure 10.11

Since chorale writing is for the human voice, we need to know the limits and ranges of each part. Voices are as individual as fingerprints. Individual singers vary, and factors like dynamic level can influence a singers range. Figure 10.12 shows the approximate, average ranges for each voice category. You should keep your writing within these voice ranges.

Figure 10.12

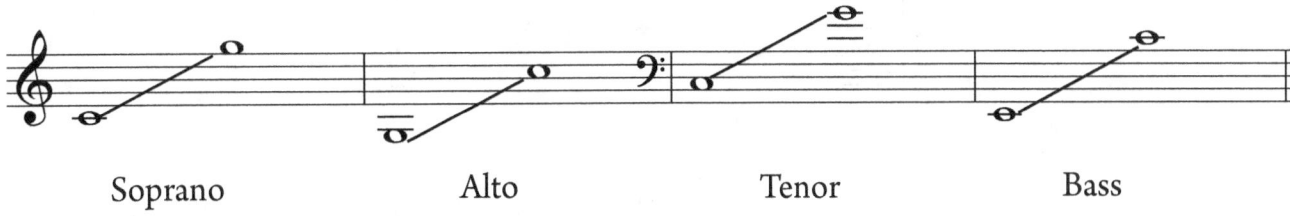

Study the following steps for writing an authentic cadence in chorale style in G minor.

1. Add the key signature and rests at the beginning of the first measure. Add functional chord symbols indicating the authentic cadence (V - i). Write the bass notes for the V and i chord in G minor (Figure 10.13).

Figure 10.13

V   i

2. Write the notes of the V chord with doubled root in G minor. V contains the raised leading tone (DF#AD). It might help to write the letter names of the chord under the staff. Be sure to use the correct stem direction and proper spacing between the voices. The space between the top three voices must not exceed one octave (Figure 10.14).

Figure 10.14

V   i

(D F# A D)

3. Write the notes of the i chord with doubled root in G minor. Repeat the common tone (D) in the same voice. Here, it is in the soprano. Move the other voices as smoothly as possible from the V chord to the i chord. In an authentic cadence with a common tone, the remaining two voices step up from the V to the i chord (F# to G and A to B♭) (Figure 10.15).

Figure 10.15

V   i

(D F# A D) (G B♭ D G)

1. Add the alto and tenor to create authentic cadences in chorale style. (The first one is completed for you).

- It may help to write the letter names of the chord tones under each chord.
- Repeat the common tone in the same voice.
- Move the other voices as closely as possible, preferably by step.
- In minor keys, raise the leading tone in chord V. If the leading tone is in the soprano it must step up to the tonic.
- Be careful of spacing. Do not allow more than one octave space between the top 3 voices.

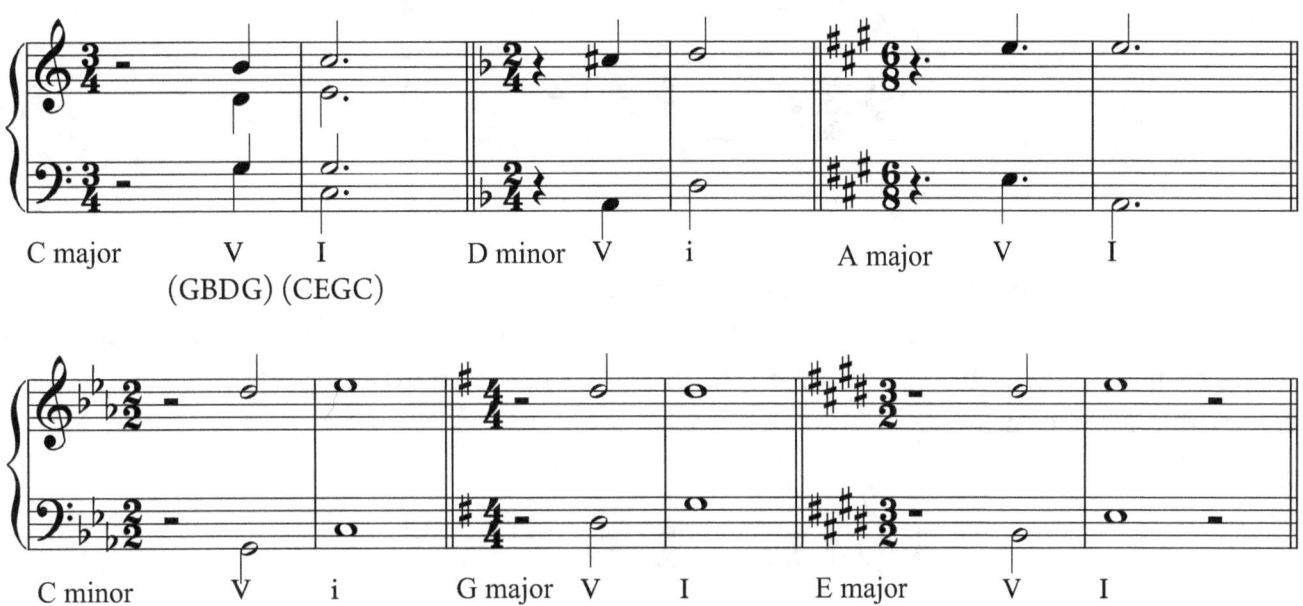

2. Complete the following authentic cadences by adding the tonic chord.

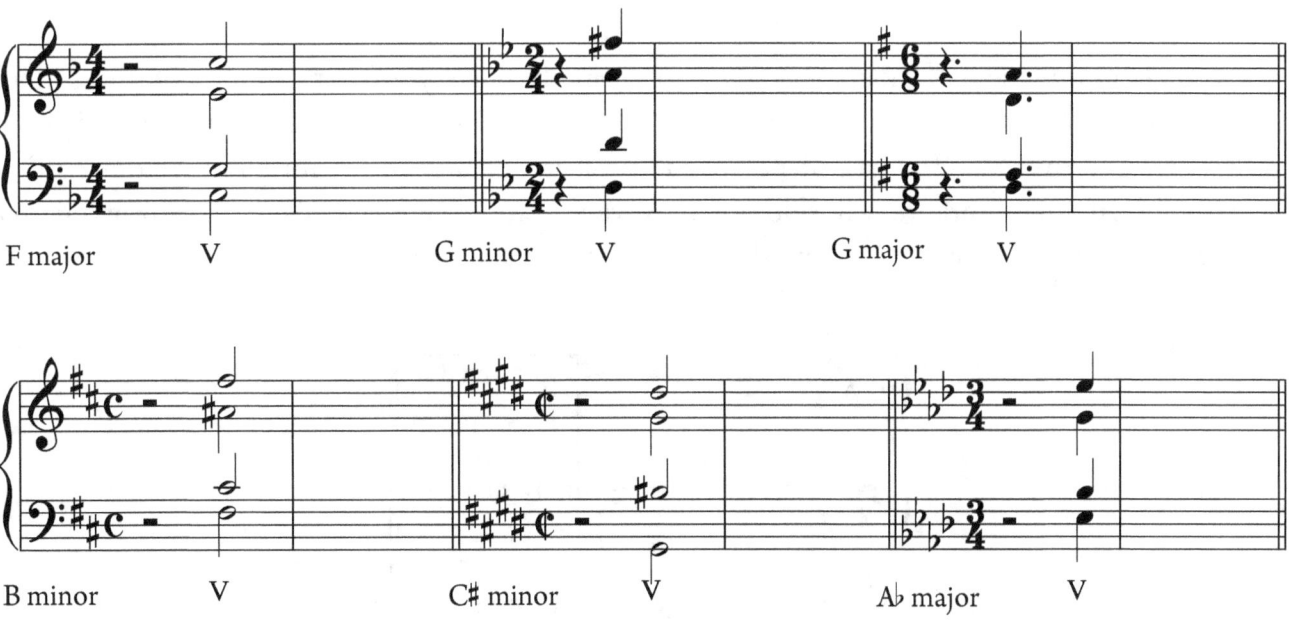

Cadences

Figure 10.16 is a plagal cadence written in chorale style. Writing this cadence is similar to writing the authentic cadence.

- Repeat the common tone in the same voice.
- Move the remaining voices of the IV chord to the nearest available chord tones of the I chord.

In this example the common tone (C) is repeated in the soprano. The bass moves from the root of IV (F) to the root of I (C). The alto and tenor fall a step.

Figure 10.16

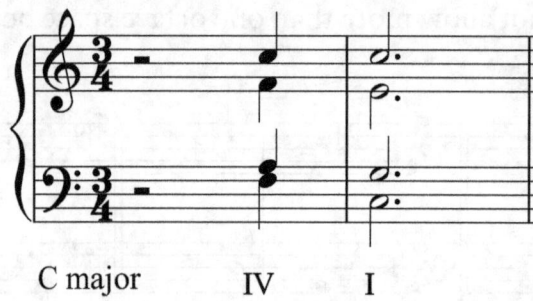

C major   IV   I

Figure 10.17 is a half cadence written in chorale style. In this example, the bass moves from the root of I (C) to the root of V (G). The common tone (G) is repeated in the tenor. The remaining voices move down by step. Always try to move to the nearest available chord tone and avoid any awkward leaps within a voice part.

Figure 10.17

C major   I   V

Figure 10.18 contains the half cadence IV - V written in chorale style. There are no common tones in this cadence. When writing this cadence, it is important to move the three upper voices in contrary motion to the bass. The bass steps up, so the soprano, alto, and tenor all move down. Two voices will step down, and one will skip down. Always write the bass in this cadence moving up a step. The alternative is down a 7th, and this melodic interval is awkward.

Figure 10.18

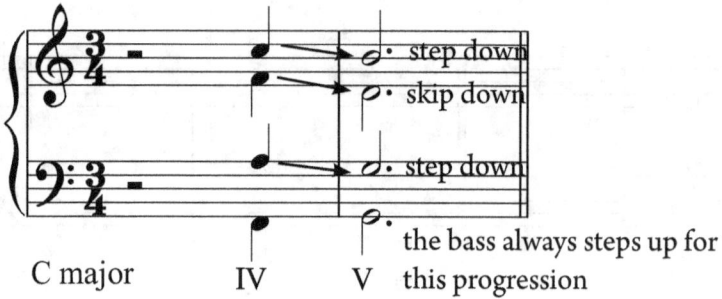

C major   IV   V

1. Write the following cadences in chorale style.

a. An authentic cadence in G major
b. A plagal cadence in C minor
c. A half cadence (I - V) in B♭ major
d. An authentic cadence in D minor
e. A half cadence (iv - V) in A minor
f. A plagal cadence in E major
g. A half cadence (i - V) in F♯ minor
h. An authentic cadence in F minor
i. A half cadence (IV - V) in D major

Cadences

2. Name the key. Write an appropriate cadence in chorale style at the end of the following phrases. Add the functional chord symbols and name the cadences.

Key:_____   Cadence:_____

Cadence:_____

Key:_____   Cadence:_____

Cadence:_____

3. Name the key. Write an appropriate cadence in keyboard style at the end of the following phrases. Add the functional chord symbols and name the cadences.

Key:_____   Cadence:_____

                                                 Cadence:_____

Key:_____   Cadence:_____

                                                 Cadence:_____

11
Melody 2

Review - Implied Harmony

The notes of a melody can imply or suggest certain chords that may go along with it. This is called the ***implied harmony***. The notes of the melody in Figure 11.1 imply the primary chords I and V in the key of G major. This melody consists entirely of chord tones. V - I at the end of the phrase implies an authentic cadence. For a melody to make sense harmonically, a recognizable cadence should be suggested at the end of the phrase.

Figure 11.1

The notes of the melody in Figure 11.2 imply the chords i and V in the key of G minor. This melody contains a non-chord tone in m.1 and two non-chord tones in m.3. These notes are not part of the underlying harmony (G B♭ D). These notes are ***passing tones***. A passing tone fills in the skip between two chord tones. Passing tones are approached and left by step. A half cadence (i - V) is implied at the end of this phrase.

Figure 11.2

Study the implied harmony for the melody in Figure 11.3. Measures 3 and 4 contain non-chord tones called ***neighbor tones***. A neighbor tone is a non-chord tone that moves a step above or below a chord tone and then returns to the chord tone. Like passing tones, they are approached and left by step.

Figure 11.3

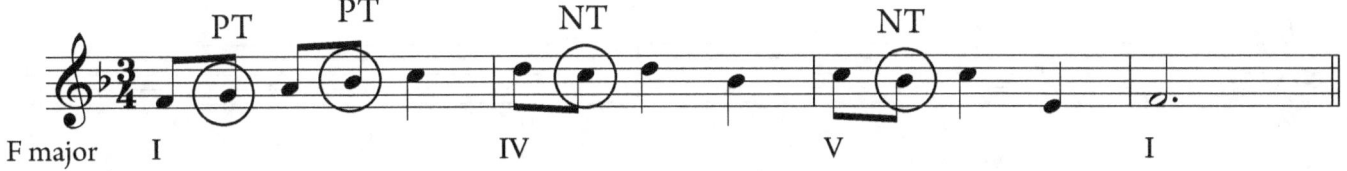

1. Name the key and state implied harmony by adding functional chord symbols to the following melodies. Circle and identify any non-chord tones.

Key:_____

Key:_____

Key:_____

Key:_____

2. Name the key and state implied harmony by adding functional chord symbols to the following melodies. Rewrite the melodies adding passing and neighbor tones.

Key:_____

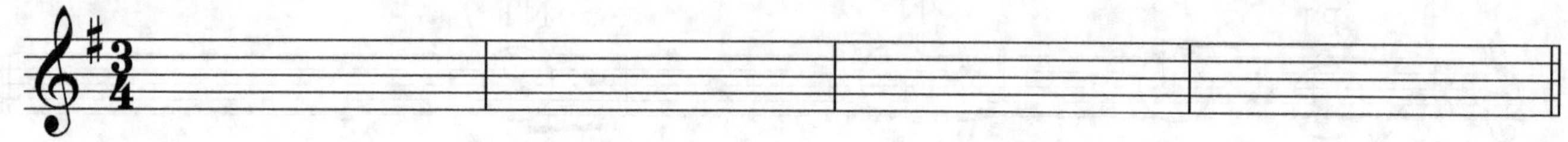

Key:_____

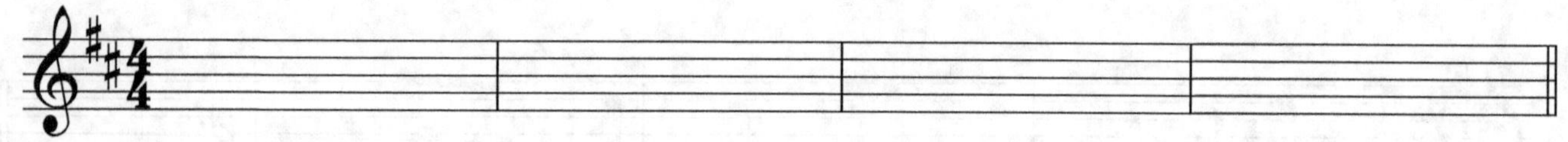

Minor Key Melodies

Avoid writing augmented intervals melodically. They are dissonant intervals and do not sound good in a melody. Two augmented intervals to be aware of are shown in Figure 11.4.

1. An augmented 2nd occurs between $\hat{6}$ and raised $\hat{7}$ in minor keys when using the harmonic minor scale.
2. An augmented 4th occurs in both major and minor keys between $\hat{4}$ and $\hat{7}$.

Figure 11.4

D minor   C major

The D minor melody in Figure 11.5 contains two augmented 2nds between the submediant ($\hat{6}$) and the leading tone ($\sharp\hat{7}$). These should be avoided.

Figure 11.5

Figure 11.6 is a better version of the same melody using the melodic form of the minor scale. In m.2 the descending form of D melodic minor is used with the subtonic ($\hat{7}$) and submediant ($\hat{6}$). In m.3 the ascending form of D melodic minor is used with the raised submediant ($\natural\hat{6}$) and leading tone ($\sharp\hat{7}$). This eliminates the augmented 2nds.

Here, the descending version of the melodic minor scale was used for notes that were going down, and the ascending version was used for notes going up. However, it is fine to use the descending version for notes going up and vice versa. In either case, the augmented 2nd is avoided.

Figure 11.6

Study the two phrase melody in Figure 11.7. The implied harmony is stated using functional chord symbols. It is crucial that your melodies make harmonic sense. The first phrase ends on an unstable scale degree ($\hat{2}$), supporting a half cadence. The second phrase ends on a stable scale degree ($\hat{1}$) supporting an authentic cadence. The non-chord tones are passing tones and neighbor tones. Circle and label the non-chord tones in these phrases.

Figure 11.7

1. Complete the following melodic fragments using the given implied harmony to create four bar melodies in minor keys. End each melody on a stable tone. Name the key of each.

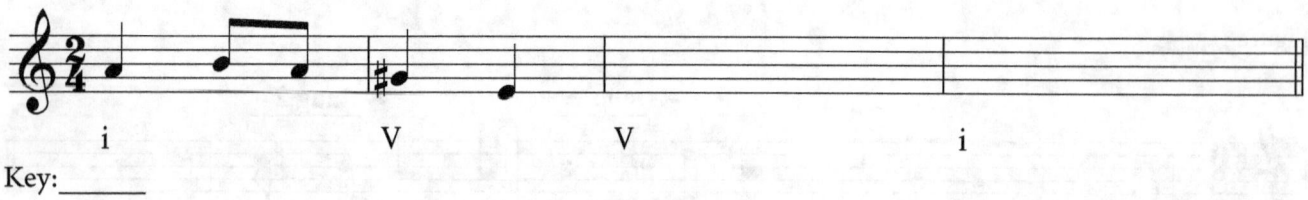

Key:_____

Key:_____

Key:_____

Key:_____

2. Complete the following melodic fragments using the given implied harmony to create four bar melodies in minor keys. End each melody on an unstable scale degree implying a half cadence. Name the key of each.

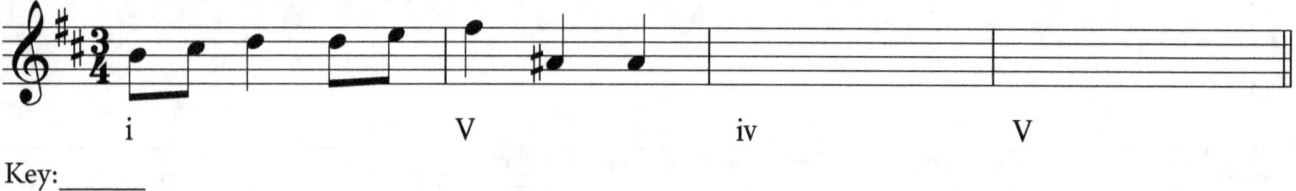

Key:_____

Key:_____

12

History 2

The Renaissance Era (ca 1450 - 1600)

The Renaissance Era (ca. 1450-1600) brought about great change in both sacred and secular music. For most of the Medieval Era, music was reserved for the Church and the wealthy. Advancements and social changes in the Renaissance Era allowed music to flourish in both sacred and secular genres. Despite the Reformation and the Counter Reformation, there was continuous musical growth happening in both the Catholic and the Protestant Churches.

In the Renaissance, the motet and the Mass were the most common forms of sacred music. However, many forms of secular music were being developed. Secular music included *madrigals*, which were part songs for several voices, and the rise of both instrumental and dance music.

Josquin Des Prez (ca 1440 - 1521)

Josquin des Prez, from the Renaissance era, became known as one of the greatest composers of the 16th century. He is often just called Josquin. Josquin's date and place of birth are not known, but he was probably born between 1440 and 1450 in France or Belgium. As an adult, he enjoyed a successful musical career in Italy.

Josquin's specialties included the use of overlapping vocals, as found in the canon or round, which is a composition of overlapping vocals in the strictest sense. Using these techniques allowed Josquin to be extremely expressive in the setting of text, while also enriching its meaning. Josquin Des Prez is regarded as one of the leading composers of Renaissance choral music. His compositions are still performed throughout the world today.

El Grillo

"*El Grillo*," or "The Cricket," is a light, fun, *a cappella* piece by Josquin. A cappella refers to vocal music without instrumental accompaniment. El Grillo is considered a *frottola*. This is a polyphonic vocal work, and an ancestor of the madrigal. Josquin wrote three frottole and El Grillo is his most popular. It is written for four voices. The text is in Italian. The English translation of the lyrics are:

> The cricket is a good singer
> Who can hold a long note
> Of drinking the cricket sings
> The cricket is a good singer
> But he doesn't do what birds do,
> After they've sung a bit,
> They go somewhere else,
> The cricket always stays put
> And when the weather is hottest
> He sings solely for love

Josquin uses *word painting* in this piece. Word painting was common in the Renaissance, as the madrigal became popular. Word painting is when the music matches the meaning of the word. For example, on the line "Who can hold a long note," the word "long" is extended. At one point in the refrain, the voices are meant to mimic the chirp of a cricket.

In portions of El Grillo, Josquin uses *homorhythm*. This is a texture where all parts sing in the same rhythm. This rhythm results in a blocked chordal texture. Homorhythmic texture allows the lyrics to be very clear and easy to understand. Figure 12.1 contains the opening measures of El Grillo.

Figure 12.1

Review 2

1. Name the following intervals. Invert each interval in the bass clef and rename it.

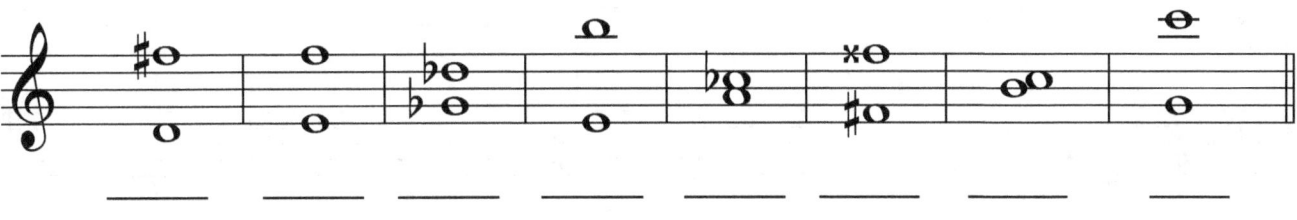

2. Add rests under the brackets to complete each measure.

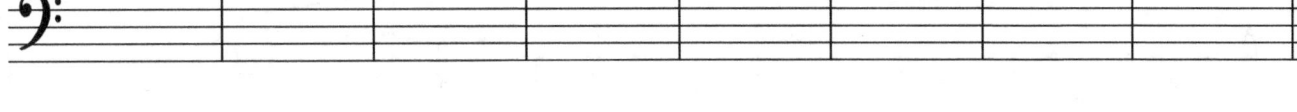

3. Add barlines to the following according to the time signature.

4. For the following melodies. Name the key. Write a cadence in chorale style at the end of each phrase. Add functional chord symbols for the cadence and name the type of cadence.

Key:_____   Cadence:_____

Key:_____   Cadence:_____

5. Give the root/quality chord symbol for the following chords.

a. the dominant 7th of D major in root position   **A⁷**

b. the supertonic triad of B♭ major in root position   _____

c. the mediant triad of A major in root position   _____

d. the leading tone triad of F major in 1st inversion   _____

e. the diminished 7th of B harmonic minor   _____

6. Define the following German terms

    sehr _____

    mit Ausdruck _____

    mässig _____

    langsam _____

    schnell _____

    bewegt _____

7. For the following minor key melodic fragments: Name the key. Complete the remaining two measures creating a phrase that ends on a stable scale degree (preferably 1̂).

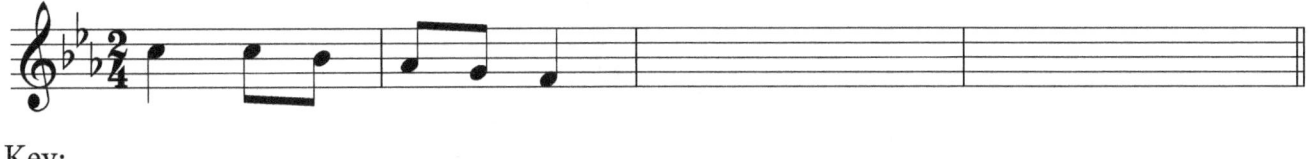

Key:_____

Key:_____

8. Match the composition (or compositions) that best apply to the following statements.

a. **Ordo Virtutum**	b. **Sumer Is Icumen In**	c. **El Grillo**

Composed by Hildegard von Bingen   _____

An example of a 'frottola'   _____

Monophonic texture   _____

A 'rota"   _____

Contains an ostinato or 'pes'   _____

Polyphonic composition for 4 voices   _____

Composed by Josquin des Prez   _____

Composed in the Medieval era   _____

Uses word painting   _____

An example of plainchant   _____

Uses homorhythm   _____

Latin text   _____

Italian text   _____

Composed in the Renaissance era   _____

Polyphonic composition for 6 voices   _____

13
Transposition

Review - Transposing by Interval or Key

To transpose a melody up by a major 2nd:

1. Determine the key of the given melody. Figure 13.1 is in F major. The B♮ is an accidental.

Figure 13.1

2. A major 2nd above F is G. The new key will be G major. Write the key signature of G major (F♯), the time signature, and move every note up a 2nd (Figure 13.2).

Figure 13.2

3. Look at the accidentals in the original melody. In the original the melody one B♭ was raised a half step to B♮ (Figure 13.3).

Figure 13.3

4. Insert the corresponding accidental in the transposed melody. Here, the C must be raised a half step to C♯ (Figure 13.4).

Figure 13.4

If a melody is in a minor key, the transposed melody will also be in a minor key. The melody in Figure 13.5 is in A minor.

Figure 13.5

A minor

If we transpose the melody in Figure 13.5 down a major 3rd, the new key will be F minor. F to A is a major 3rd. Even though we are transposing by a major interval, the original melody is minor, so the transposed melody must be minor. Add tempo and dynamic markings.

Figure 13.6 shows the melody transposed into the key of F minor.

Figure 13.6

F minor

If you are asked to transpose a melody into a specific key, determine the interval of transposition first. To transpose the melody in Figure 13.5 into the key of D minor, you could transpose it up a perfect 4th (A up to D is a per 4th), or down a perfect 5th (D down to A is a per 5th). Both would be correct. Write the key signature of D minor and move the notes up a 4th or down 5th. Add any necessary accidentals. Figure 13.7 shows the melody transposed down into the key of D minor.

Figure 13.7

D minor

1. Name the key and transpose the following melodies as indicated. Name the new keys where appropriate.

Up a major 3rd

Johann Sebastian Bach
WTC Bk. I, No. 12

Key: _____

Key: _____

Down a perfect 4th

Wolfgang Amadeus Mozart
Divertimento K.229, No. 2

Larghetto

Key: _____

Key: _____

Up into F# minor

Pyotr Tchaikowsky
Symphony No. 6

Key: _____

Transposing Instruments

Some instruments produce a pitch that is different than the one that is written. These instruments are known as *transposing instruments*. Suppose you write a piece for trumpet and give a copy to your friend who plays piano, to play along with you. You find the resulting sound is horrible. Why? The trumpet is a transposing instrument, and the piano is not. Not every C and D, or every note for that matter, is the same. It depends on the instrument you are playing.

Concert Pitch

The pitch of a note is created by the vibration of air. These vibrations can be measured and given a frequency number called **hertz** (Hz). Many instruments play in **concert pitch**. This means when they play a note they produce a specific frequency. When you play middle C on the piano, you produce a note with the frequency of 261 hz. This is an exact pitch, and it is associated with concert pitch. Here is a list of some of the instruments that play in concert pitch.

- Piano
- Violin, viola, cello , bass
- Guitar
- Flute, piccolo
- Harp
- Oboe
- Bassoon
- Trombone
- Pitched percussion instruments like marimba, xylophone, timpani
- Tuba

Transposing Instruments - Instruments in B flat

Transposing instruments read the same music and use the same staff, clefs and notes as concert pitch instruments. The difference is when a trumpet plays the note C, it does not register as C according to the hertz scale (261 hz) and it does not match the C on the piano. The trumpet is a B♭ instrument and when it plays C, you hear a B♭ in concert pitch, or it matches the B♭ on the piano. This is what is meant by a transposing instrument. Some B♭ instruments are:

- Trumpet
- Clarinet
- Soprano saxophone

Figure 13.8 contains a melody for B♭ trumpet. When it is played, what we hear, concert pitch, is on the second staff. Since we hear B♭ when the trumpet plays C, concert pitch is heard a major 2nd below. In this *Concerto*, a piece for trumpet and orchestra, when the trumpet plays F, we hear E♭. This trumpet concerto is in E♭ major, but the B♭ trumpet plays in F major, a major 2nd higher than concert pitch. The string section, which plays in concert pitch, is playing in E♭ major.

If you have a melody written in concert pitch and want to write it for a B♭ instrument, you have to transpose it up a major 2nd.

If you have a melody written for a B♭ instrument and want to write it in concert pitch, you have to transpose it down a major 2nd.

Figure 13.8

1. The following melody is written for clarinet in B♭. Name the key and transpose it into concert pitch. Name the new key.

Key: _____

Key: _____

2. The following melody is written in concert pitch. Name the key and transpose it for trumpet in B♭. Name the new key.

Johann Nepomuk Hummel
Trumpet Concerto, III

Key: _____

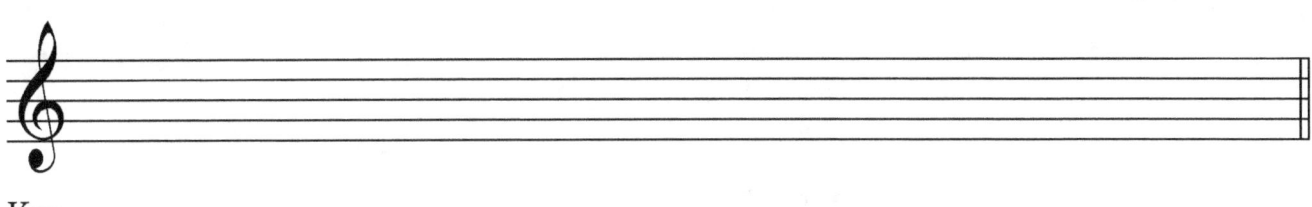

Key: _____

3. The following melody is written for clarinet in B♭. Name the key and transpose it into concert pitch. Name the new key.

Wolfgang Amadeus Mozart
Symphony No. 40, Minuet

Key: _____

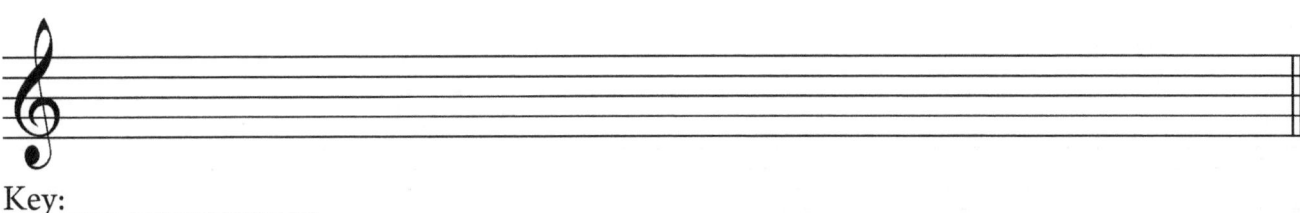

Key: _____

Transposing Instruments - Instruments in F

Two instruments transpose in the key of F:

- French horn
- English horn

They both transpose in the same manner, a fifth away. Music for these instruments must be transposed down a perfect 5th to get to concert pitch. (See Figure 13.9) In other words, a melody in concert pitch must be written up a perfect 5th to sound correct when played by an F instrument. A melody written for an F instrument must be transposed down a perfect 5th to sound correct at concert pitch.

Figure 13.9

French/English horn plays:

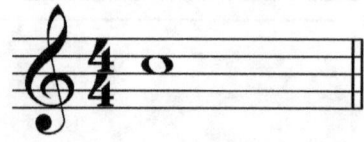

We hear at concert pitch:

1. The following melody is written for horn in F. Name the key and transpose it into concert pitch. Name the new key.

Wolfgang Amadeus Mozart
Concerto for Horn K. 447, III

Key: _____

Key: _____

2. The following examples are in concert pitch. Name the keys and rewrite each one for the instrument indicated. Name the new keys.

Wolfgang Amadeus Mozart
Allegro, K.312

Allegro

Key: _____

Clarinet in B♭

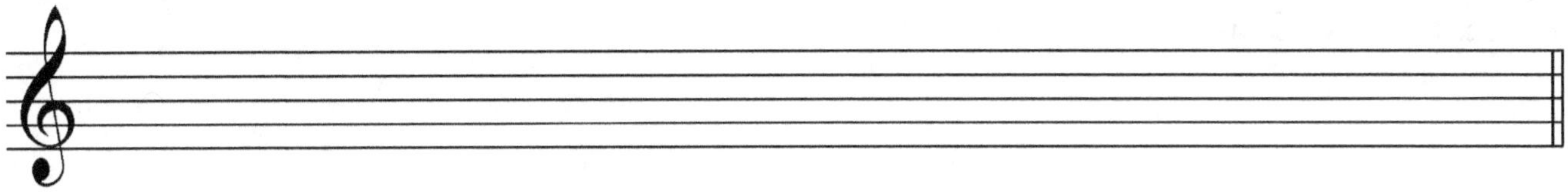

Key: _____

French Horn

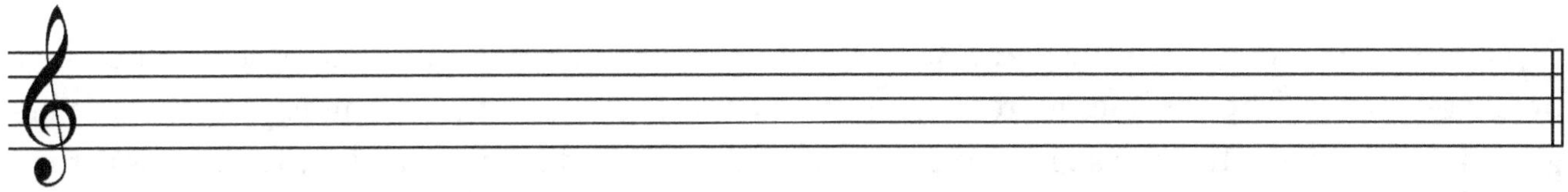

Key: _____

Antono Vivaldi
The Four Seasons, Spring

Largo

Key: _____

English Horn

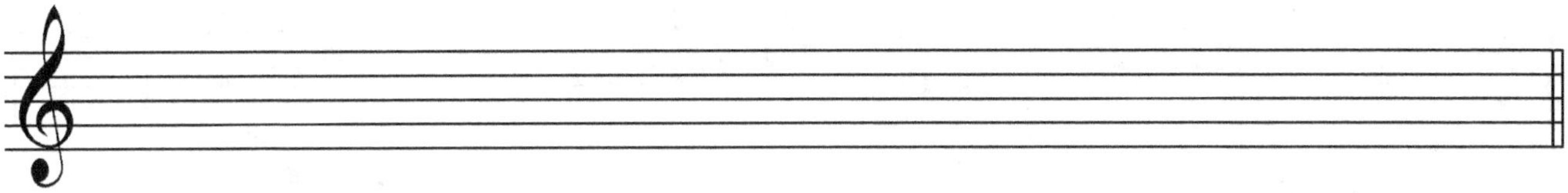

Key: _____

Trumpet in B♭

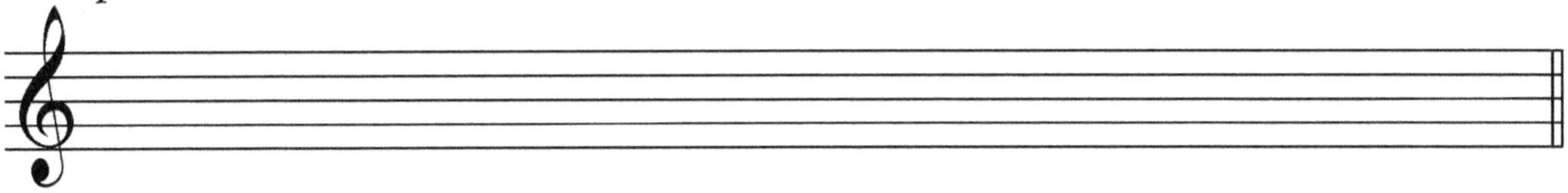

Key: _____

14
Score Types

Score is a common term for notated music. There are several types of scores which we will discuss in this lesson.

Piano Score

A piano score is written on the grand staff. It consists of the treble and the bass staff joined by a bracket or brace. The bar lines go through both staves. The tempo indication is placed at the beginning of the staff. The key signature comes after the clef and is followed by the time signature. Dynamics (fp) are placed between the two staves. Figure 14.1 is a piano score.

Figure 14.1

Orchestral Score

An orchestral score has staves for all the instruments that are playing. The instruments are placed in the following order: woodwinds, brass, percussion (timpani), strings. Each section is divided with a bracket on the left side. the instruments are placed on the staff from highest to lowest in each family. The instrument names are usually written in Italian. On this score, the English translations are included. There is one tempo mark at the beginning, and each part receives its own dynamic marking.

Figure 14.2

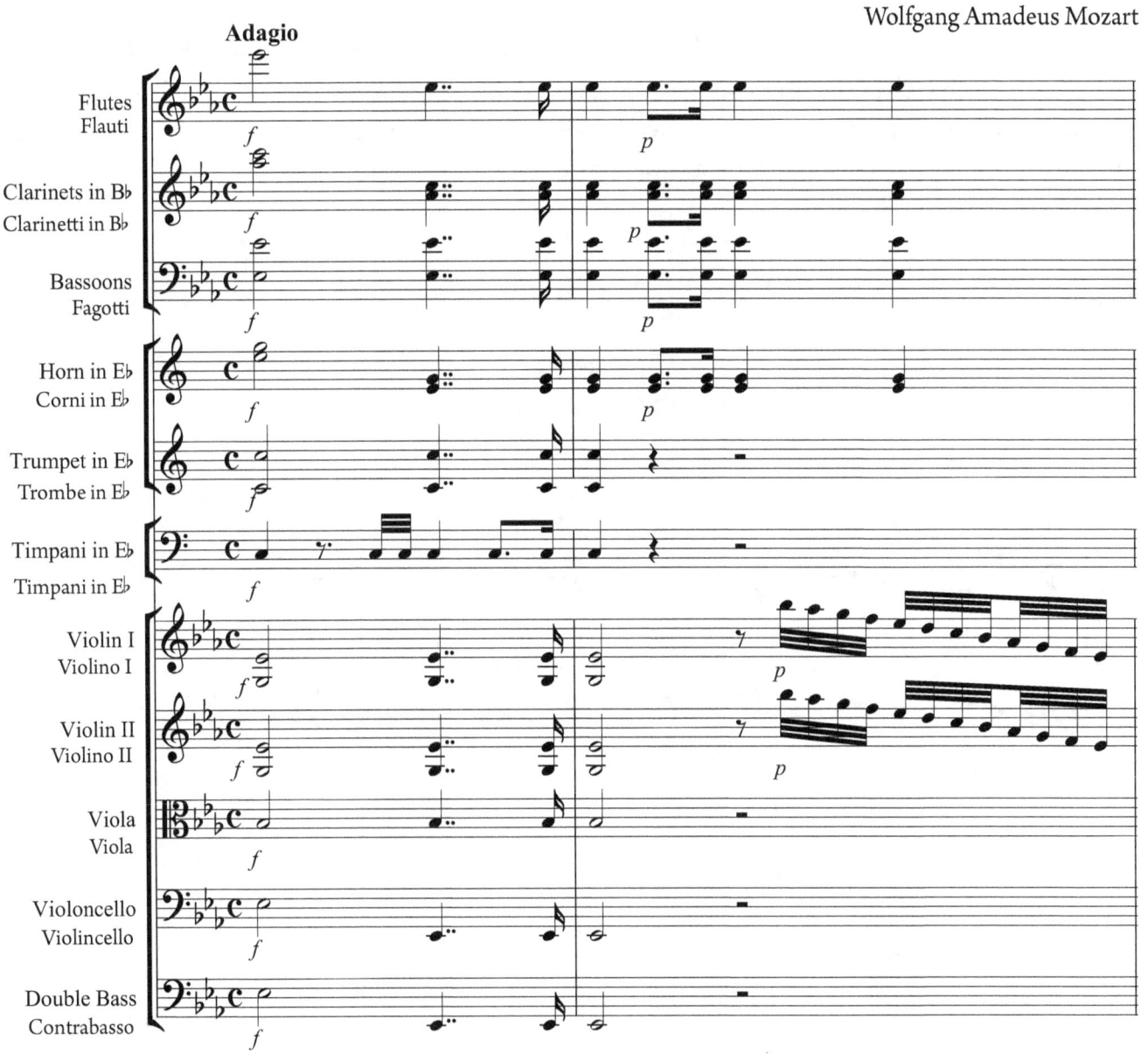

Vocal Scores

Short Score

Short score, which is sometimes called condensed score, looks a little like piano score but there are some differences. This score consists of the treble and bass staves joined at the beginning by a line and a brace. In vocal music, the bar lines do not run through the entire staff.

This score is written for the four voices of a choir: soprano, alto, tenor, and bass. The soprano and alto parts are written on the treble staff, and the tenor and bass parts ware written on the bass staff.

Stem direction rules are different in short score. The soprano stems go up, and the alto stems go down in the treble clef. The tenor stems go up, and the bass stems go down in the bass clef. This separates the parts, and each singer can clearly see their line. The text to be sung is placed between the staves. Figure 14.3 is an example of a short score.

Figure 14.3

Modern Vocal Score

Modern vocal score is an example of ***open score***. In open score, each part gets its own staff. The three upper parts are written on treble staves. The bass part is written on the bass staff. The tenor part is written one octave higher on the treble staff. Each part receives the text to be sung.

Figure 14.4 is the chorale from Figure 14.3 written in modern vocal score.

Figure 14.4

Chorale No. 293
Was Gott tut, das ist wohlgetan

Johann Sebastian Bach

S: Was Gott tut, das ist wohl - ge tan.
A: Was Gott tut, das ist wohl ge tan.
T: Was Gott tut, das ist___ wohl ge tan.
B: Was Gott tut, das ist wohl ge tan.

String Quartet Score

String quartet score is an open score. The instruments in this score are first violin, second violin, viola, and cello (violoncello). The violin parts are written using two treble staves. The viola is written using the alto staff and the cello is written using the bass staff.

Figure 14.5 is written in string quartet score. The instruments are abbreviated as:

> Vl. I
> Vl. II
> Vla
> Vc

Figure 14.5

Writing in Short and Open Score

There are few things to consider when transcribing a passage from short to open score or vice versa. The example in Figure 14.6 is in short score. The stem direction goes up for soprano and tenor and down for alto and bass. The tempo is written once, the dynamic sign is written once, and the fermata is written above the soprano and below the bass.

Figure 14.6

Figure 14.7 shows the same example written in open score for SATB. Normal rules of stem direction are followed. The tempo is written once at the top, and each part receives a dynamic marking. Each part receives a fermata. All four voices are lined up evenly on the score.

Figure 14.7

In short score, the ties in the soprano and tenor parts curve upwards, and the ties in the alto and bass parts always curve downwards. Figure 14.8 contains ties in the soprano and alto.

Figure 14.8

In open score, ties are always written on the opposite side of the note to the stem.

Figure 14.9

Sometimes, two parts can sing an identical note or a "unison," or they may sing the interval of a second.

Study the soprano and alto parts in Figure 14.10. On beat one they are singing the same G. On beat two the soprano has a G, and the alto has the F directly below it.

Figure 14.10

These parts are transcribed into short score in Figure 14.11. In a short score, a unison is shown by writing one note-head with two stems. One stem points up, and the other points down.

For the interval of a major second on beat two, the F in the alto is moved slightly to the right. This allows both notes to be seen.

Figure 14.11

1. Write the following passage in open score for a string quartet.

Johann Sebastian Bach
Chorale no. 67: Freu'dich sehr, o meine Seele

2. Write the following passage in modern vocal score.

Johann Sebastian Bach
Das walt' mein gott

3. Write the following passage in short score.

Ludwig van Beethoven
String Quartet Op 18, No. 1

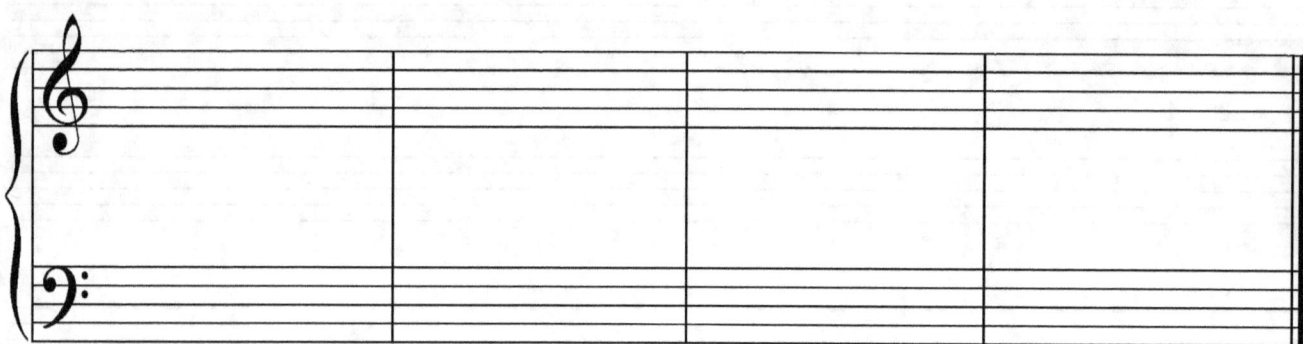

4. Write the following passage in string quartet score.

Franz Joseph Haydn
String Quartet Op 76, No. 3

5. Write the following passage in short score.

Johann Sebastian Bach
O Haupt Voll und Wunden

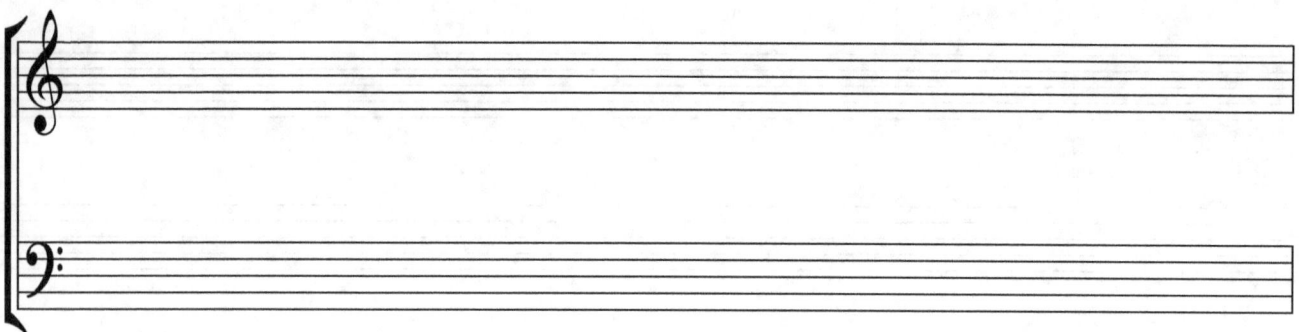

15
Melody 3

Review - Melodic Structure

A *period* is a section of music that is usually eight measures long and contains two four-measure phrases called antecedent and consequent.

Antecedent and consequent phrases are common in music. The first phrase acts as a question, often ending on an unstable tone ($\hat{2}$ or $\hat{7}$), which requires an answer. The second phrase provides the answer and usually ends on a stable tone ($\hat{1}$ or $\hat{3}$).

The melody in Figure 15.1 consists of two phrases that are almost the same. The difference is the ending. The first phrase ends on an unstable pitch ($\hat{2}$). The second phrase ends on a stable pitch ($\hat{1}$). Since the second phrase uses the same melody with a slight alteration, the two phrases are labeled a and a^1. This type of melody construction, with two similar melodies, is called a *parallel period*.

Figure 15.1

Phrases end in cadences. In Figure 15.1, the unstable pitch $\hat{2}$ (E) at the end of the first phrase implies a half cadence.
The second phrase ends on the stable pitch $\hat{1}$, implying an authentic cadence. It is important that the notes at the end of a melodic phrase imply a logical cadence.

The ***contrasting period*** consists of two differing four measure phrases labelled: **a** and **b**.
The melodic material in the second (consequent) phrase is different than **a**. For this reason, it is labeled "**b**."

Study and play the melody in Figure 15.2. There are two phrases, an antecedent, and a consequent. Section **a** and section **b** differ. Section **b** uses the same rhythm as section **a**, but it contains new melodic material. This type of melody, containing two differing phrases, is a contrasting period.

Figure 15.2

The melody in Figure 15.3, is a contrasting period. The implied harmony is indicated using functional chord symbols. Good melodies make harmonic sense and have a logical chord structure. The first phrase ends with an unstable chord tone ($\hat{2}$), implying a half cadence. The second phrase ends with a stable chord tone ($\hat{1}$), implying an authentic cadence. In the approach to the final tonic, $\hat{6}$ and $\hat{7}$ are raised. $\hat{7}$ must be raised since it is the leading tone, and $\hat{6}$ is raised to avoid an augmented second in the melody. Ending the melody on $\hat{1}$ is very strong and emphasizes the tonality. It is common to approach the final $\hat{1}$ from a step below (B♮ - C) or from a step above (D - C). This implies an authentic cadence.

Figure 15.3

1. For the following given consequent (a) phrases:

   - Name the key.
   - Write an antecedent phrase (b) creating a contrasting period.
   - Use the suggested implied harmony as a guideline. Alter it if you wish, but end the phrase with a logical authentic cadence. It may help to end on $\hat{1}$, approached from a step below ($\hat{7}$-$\hat{1}$) or a step above ($\hat{2}$-$\hat{1}$).

2. For the following melodic fragments:

   - Name the key.
   - Complete the consequent (a) phrase, ending on an unstable scale degree ($\hat{2}$, $\hat{7}$, $\hat{5}$).
   - Write an antecedent (b) phrase creating a contrasting period ending on a stable scale degree ($\hat{1}$).
   - State the implied harmony using functional chord symbols.

Key:_____

Key:_____

Key:_____

16
History 3

Global Music - The Javanese Gamelan

In 1899, French composer Claude Debussy, upon hearing a Javanese gamelan orchestra wrote: 'Their conservatory is the rhythm of the sea, the wind among the leaves and the thousand sounds of nature...'. For centuries, Indonesians have developed their gamelan orchestras, making sounds that are other worldly, magical, yet still human all at the same time. Since Debussy, other nations have been fascinated and intrigued by this music, and it has spread throughout the world.

The word '**gamelan**' is derived from the Indonesian word meaning 'hammer.' A gamelan is an Indonesian mallet orchestra native to Bali and Java. The gamelan orchestra is made up of several types of mallet instruments like the **metallophone**, a xylophone-like instrument with metal bars struck by mallets, or keyboard-style instruments struck with mallets or hammers, as well as different drums, flutes, and occasionally stringed instruments or vocalists.

Gamelan instruments are tuned differently than those in Western music. There are two tuning systems that gamelan orchestras use, one which consists of five notes, and one which has seven notes. Many of the same instruments occur in pairs, with each one being tuned slightly differently than the other. When two of the same instruments play a note in unison, the different sound waves vibrate against each other, creating a quality of sound gamelan musicians call *ombak*, or 'shimmering sound.'

Traditional Javanese gamelan music is divided into two parts: a central melody, and a part that embellishes that central melody. Gamelan music is not written down or notated. It is handed down orally (or aurally) from generation to generation.

Search the internet for videos and recordings of Gamelan orchestras.

Indian Music - The Raga

Much of Western music is based on modes, especially the major and minor modes. A **raga** is a mode (scale) found in Indian classical music and used in improvised performances. There are over 300 ragas.

Raga means 'color.' Just as each color in the spectrum is unique, each raga has a unique sound. The sound of each raga is associated with certain emotions, times of day, Hindu deities, and seasons. Ragas often use **microtones**. These are smaller intervals than those found in Western music. The traditional half step may be subdivided into quarter steps or quarter tones.

Indian classical music is improvised, so each performance is different. Despite this, Indian musicians do not play whatever they want. Their improvisations must follow the rules of the raga.

Each raga contains:

- the raga scale, which contains the specific pitches used in the piece.
- the Arohana, an ascending form of the scale.
- the Avarohana, a descending form of the scale, which may not be the same as the Arohana.
- the Vadi, an important note that is played more frequently than other notes.
- the Samvadi, a note of seconday importance.

All of these elements work together to form a larger melody called the **chalan**. When musicians master the chalan, they use it as a basis for their improvisation.

The number of instruments in a raga may vary, but there are at least three instruments involved in a performance: a drone, a drummer, and one or more melody instruments. The melody instrument plays the raga. One of the most common Indian melody instruments is the **sitar**, a long-necked, guitar-like, string instrument with a gourd-shaped resonance chamber.

The main percussion instruments used in North India are called **tabla**, a pair of drums that are tuned to work with the notes of the raga. The drums often introduce a regular rhythmic cycle called a **tala**. Tala means 'clap' and is a rhythmic beat that keeps the time of the raga.

The drone instrument is often a **tanpura**. The tanpura looks like a sitar, but has only four strings and is missing the gourd-like resonance chamber. These strings are tuned to the first and fifth scale notes and are played continuously to act as a reference point for the person playing the melody. This helps the soloist stay on track throughout their improvisation.

Find and listen to examples of Indian Raga music on the internet.

Sitar

Tabla

Tanpura

Music Terms

Study the following Italian terms and their meanings.

allargando, allarg.	getting slower and broader
arco	for strings, return to bowing after pizzicato or col legno
attacca	begin immediately, proceed without a break
calando	becoming slower and softer
comodo	at a comfortable tempo
con sordino	with the use of a mute
largamente	broadly
l'istesso tempo	at the same tempo
pizzicato	pluck the strings, for string instruments
ritenuto, riten.	suddenly slower
stringendo	gradually faster, pressing forward

Review 3

1. Name the key of the following melodies. Transpose each melody to concert pitch. Name the new key.

Carl Maria von Weber
Clarinet Concerto No.. 1

Clarinet in B♭

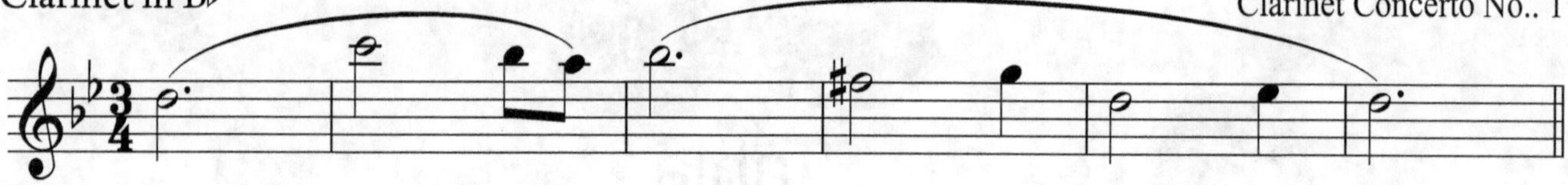

Key:_____

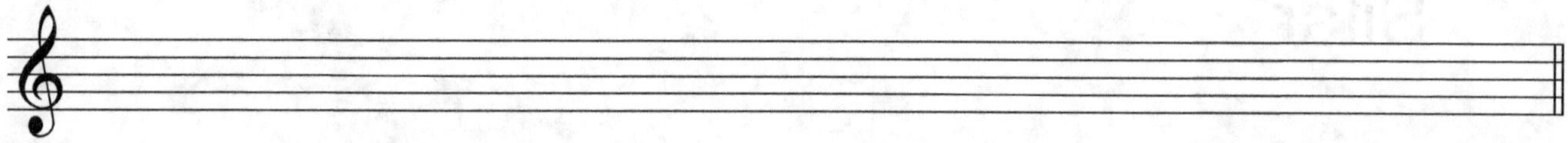

Key:_____

Wolfgang Amadeus Mozart
Adagio for 2 Horns and Bassoon

Horn in F

Key:_____

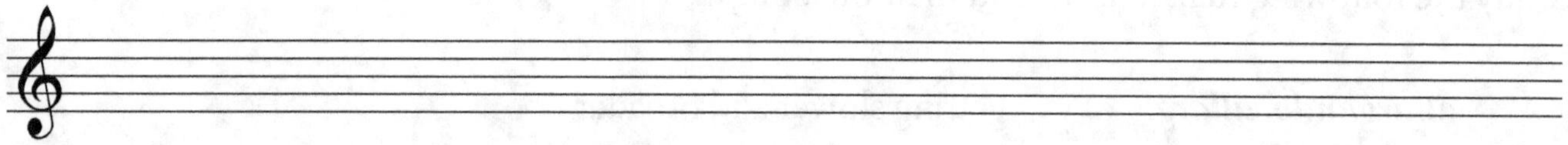

Key:_____

2. The following melody is in concert pitch. Name the key and transpose it into the correct key for English horn. Name the new key.

Wolfgang Amadeus Mozart
Concerto for Horn and Orchestra

Key:_____

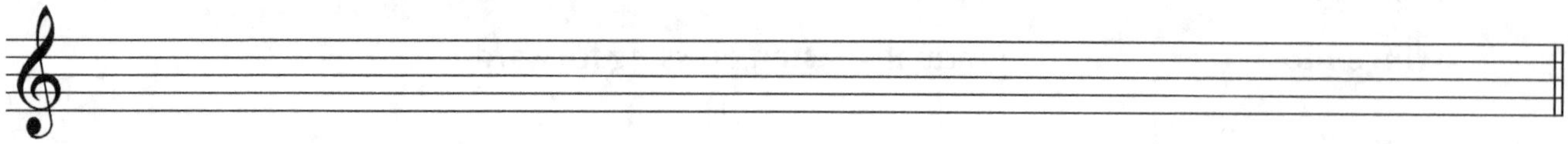

Key:_____

3. Name the key and write the functional chord symbols for the following chord progressions. Transcribe the progressions into the indicated score type.

Transcribe to modern vocal score

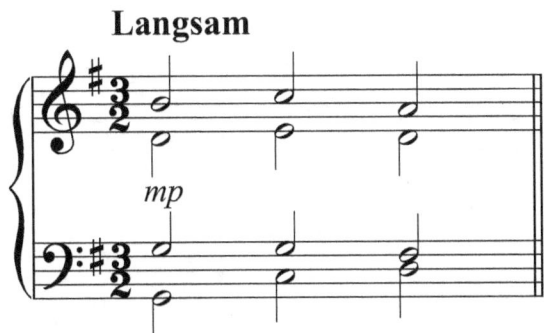

Transcribe to string quartet score

4. Write the Italian term for the following definitions.

pluck the strings, for string instruments   _____

at a comfortable tempo   _____

gradually faster, pressing forward   _____

for strings, return to bowing after pizzicato or col legno   _____

with the use of a mute   _____

suddenly slower   _____

5. For the following melodic fragment:
   - Name the key.
   - Complete the consequent (a) phrase, ending on an unstable scale degree.
   - Write an antecedent (b) phrase creating a conrasting period.
   - Name each cadence.

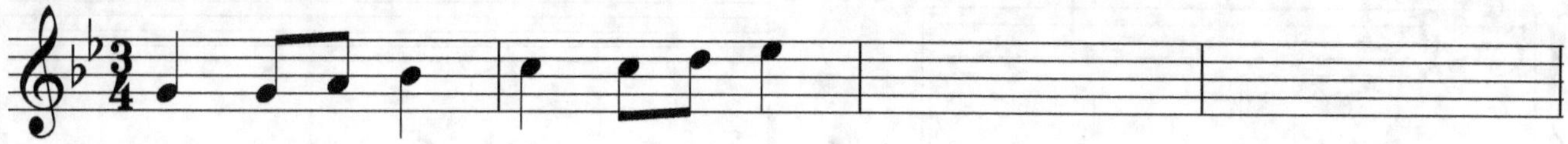

Key:_____

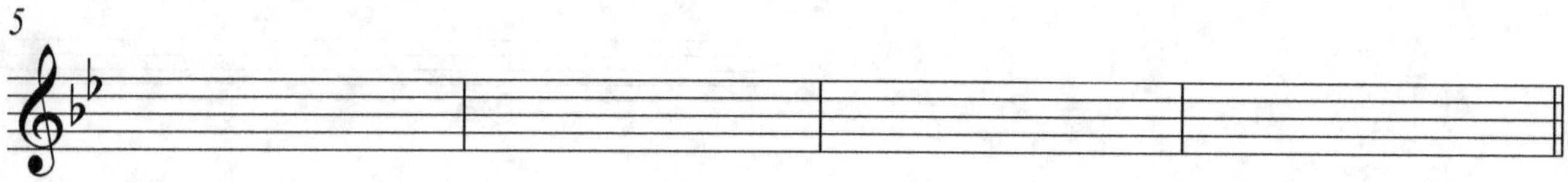

6. Define the following:

a. gamelan _____
_____
_____
_____

*b. metallophone*_____

*c. raga*_____

*d. microtone*_____

*e. tabla*_____

*f. tala*_____

17
Form and Analysis

1. For the given musical excerpt, answer the questions that follow.

Sensucht nach dem Fruhling

Wolfgang Amadeus Mozart
(1756- 1791)

a. Name the key of this piece. _____

b. Write the time signature directly on the score.

c. In what musical period was this piece composed? _____

d. Mark the phrases directly on the score.

e. Is this an example of a: ❑ parallel period   ❑ contrasting period

f. Mark the form on the score using the letters **a**, **a¹**, or **b**.

g. State the implied harmony using functional and root/quality chord symbols.

h. Circle and identify any non-chord tones.

2. For the given musical excerpt, answer the questions that follow.

Sonatina
III

Matthew Camidge
(1758- 1844)

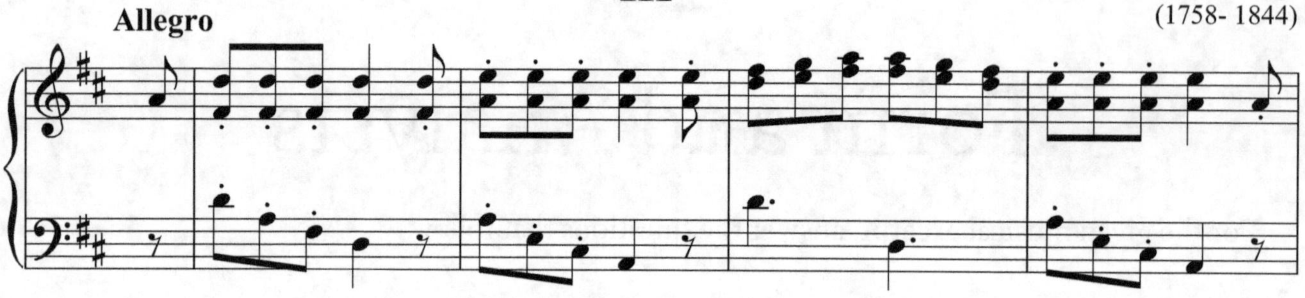

Allegro

cadence:_____

cadence:_____

a. Name the key of this piece. _____

b. Write the time signature directly on the score.

c. In what musical period was this piece composed? _____

d. Mark the phrases directly on the score.

e. Is this an example of a: ❑ parallel period   ❑ contrasting period

f. Mark the form on the score using the letters **a**, **a¹**, or **b**.

g. State the implied harmony using functional and root/quality chord symbols.

h. Circle and identify any non-chord tones.

i. Write the name of the cadences at the end of each phrase in the place provided on the score.

©San Marco Publications 2022

Form and Analysis

Voice Leading

Voice leading is concerned with the horizontal or linear aspect of music and is as important as the vertical or chordal aspect. Voice leading is very important in polyphonic music since it consists of the performance of more than one melody at the same time. Examples of this can be found in the Two-Part Inventions of J.S. Bach which were studied earlier.

There are four types of motion that can occur between two voices horizontally.

1. ***Contrary motion*** occurs when two voices move in the opposite direction. Figure 17.1 shows voices moving in contrary motion.

Figure 17.1

2. ***Oblique motion*** occurs when one voice is stationary, while the second voice moves to another pitch (up or down). Figure 17.2 shows voices moving in oblique motion.

Figure 17.2

3. ***Similar motion*** occurs when two voices move in the same direction (up or down), but not by the same interval. Figure 17.3 shows voices moving in similar motion.

Figure 17.3

4. ***Parallel motion*** occurs when two voices move in the same direction (up or down), by the same basic interval. Figure 17.4 shows voices moving in parallel motion.

Figure 17.4

5. ***Static motion*** occurs when two voices hold their notes and repeat. Actually there is no motion happening at all, only repetition. Figure 17.5 shows voices in static motion.

Figure 17.5

1. List the type of motion in each example. Contrary, oblique, similar, static, or parallel.

Study the voice leading in Figure 17.6. Both (a) and (b) are examples of parallel motion. However, there is a difference. The intervals in (a) are a major 6th and a minor 6th, while the intervals in (b) are both major 6ths. The term parallel motion does not always mean the intervals are exactly the same. The *number* is the same, but the *quality* can be different. Both intervals move in parallel motion but technically (b) is more parallel than (a). The term parallel motion does not take into account the quality of the interval.

Figure 17.6

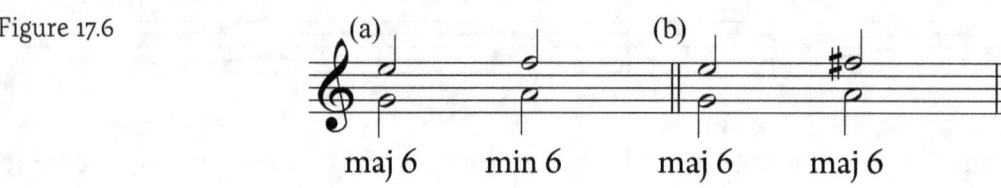

In traditional harmony and counterpoint, certain parallel perfect intervals are forbidden. These intervals are parallel perfect 5ths, parallel perfect octaves, and parallel perfect unisons. These intervals are very consonant, and when they move in parallel motion, they can lose their individual identity. The first three examples of parallel motion in Figure 17.7 should be avoided. However, a diminished 5th followed by a perfect 5th is fine.

Figure 17.7

1. The following voices move in parallel motion. Mark the correct examples with ✓ and the incorrect examples with ✗.

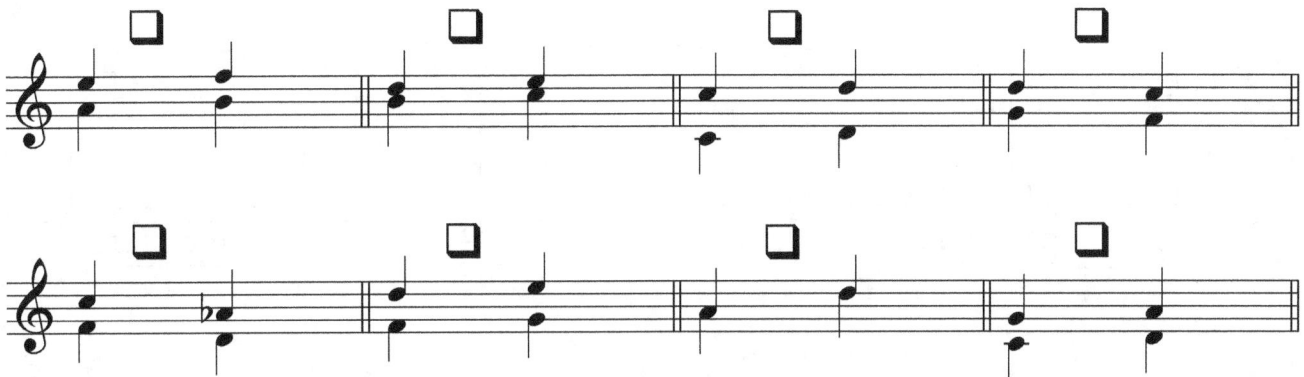

2. Answer the questions that deal with the following musical examples.

Franz Joseph Haydn
Op.74, No. 3

a. Name the key of this phrase. _____

b. Write the time signature directly on the score.

c. In what musical period was this piece composed? _____

d. What open score is this written for? _____

e. State the implied harmony using functional and root/quality chord symbols on the score.

f. Find and circle a melodic sequence.

g. Name the cadence at the end of this phrase. _____

Passepied

George Frideric Handel
(1685-1759)

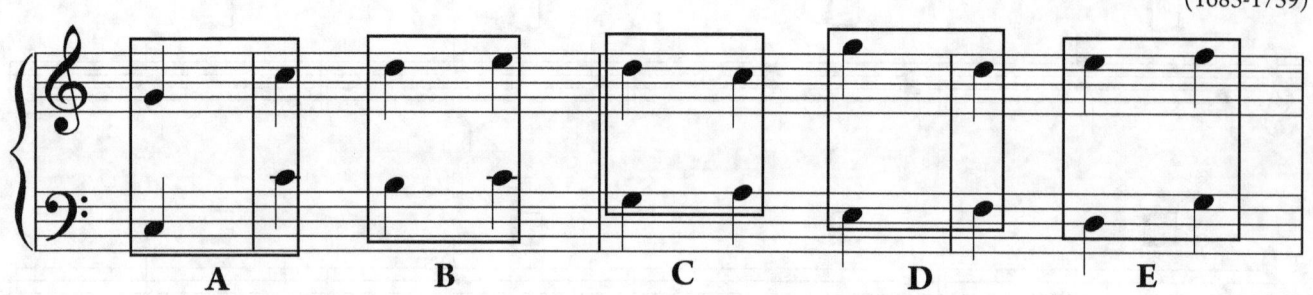

a. Add the correct time signature directly on the music.

b. Name the key of this piece._____

c. Name the composer of this piece. _____

d. Name another composition by this composer. _____

d. In what musical era was this composed? _____

e. This piece is: ❑ monophonic   ❑ polyphonic

f. Identify the motion at:

        A: ❑ contrary   ❑ parallel   ❑ similar   ❑ oblique

        B: ❑ contrary   ❑ parallel   ❑ similar   ❑ oblique

        C: ❑ contrary   ❑ parallel   ❑ similar   ❑ oblique

        D: ❑ contrary   ❑ parallel   ❑ similar   ❑ oblique

        E: ❑ contrary   ❑ parallel   ❑ similar   ❑ oblique

        F: ❑ contrary   ❑ parallel   ❑ similar   ❑ oblique

Music Terms and Signs

Terms

accelerando, accel.	becoming quicker
accent	a stressed note
ad libitum, ad lib.	at the liberty of the performer
adagio	slow
agitato	agitated
alla, all'	in the manner of
allargando	getting slower and broader
allegretto	fairly fast, a little slower than allegro
allegro	fast
andante	moderately slow, at a walking pace
andantino	a little faster than andante
animato	lively, animated
arco	for strings return to bowing after pizzicato or col legno.
attacca	begin immediately, proceed without a break
a tempo	return to the original tempo
ben, bene	well
bewegt	with movement, agitated
calando	becoming slower and softer
cantabile	in a singing style
cédez	yield, slow down
col, coll', colla, colle	with
comodo	at a comfortable tempo
con	with
con brio	with vigor
con espressione	with expression
con fuoco	with fire
con grazia	with grace
con moto	with motion
con sordino	with the use of a mute

crescendo, cresc.	becoming louder
da capo, D.C.	from the beginning
D.C. al fine	repeat from the beginning and end at *Fine*
dal segno, D.S. 𝄋	from the sign
decrescendo, decresc.	becoming softer
diminuendo, dim.	becoming softer
dolce	sweetly, gentle
dolente	sad
e, ed	and
espressivio, espress.	expressive, with expression
fine	the end
forte, f	loud
fortissimo, ff	very loud
fortepiano, fp	loud, then suddenly soft
giocoso	humorous, joyful
grandioso	grand, play in a grand and noble style
grazioso	gracefully
grave	slow and solemn
langsam	slowly
largamente	broadly
larghetto	fairly slow, not as slow as largo
largo	very slow
léger	lightly
leggiero	light
lentement	slowly
lento	slow
l'istesso tempo	at the same tempo
loco	return to the normal register
ma	but
maestoso	majestically
mano destra, m.d.	right hand

mano sinistra, m.s.	left hand
marcato	play marked or stressed
martellato	strongly accented, hammered
mässig	moderately
meno	less
meno mosso	less motion
mesto	sad, mournful
mezzo forte, mf	moderately loud
mezzo piano, mp	moderately soft
mit Ausdruck	with expression
moderato	at a moderate tempo
modéré	at a moderate tempo
molto	much, very
morendo	dying, fading away
mouvement	movement, tempo, motion
non	not
ottava, 8va	the interval of an octave
pesante	heavy, play with weight
pedale, ped	pedal
pianissimo, pp	very soft
piano, p	soft
piu	more
piu mosso	more motion
pizzicato	pluck the strings, for string instruments
poco	little
poco a poco	little by little
prestissimo	as fast as possible
presto	very fast
primo, prima	first, the upper part of a duet
quasi	almost, as if
quindicesima alta, 15ma	play 2 octaves higher

rallentando, rall.	slowing down
risoluto	resolute, bold, strong
ritardando, rit.	slowing down gradually
ritenuto, riten	suddenly slower
rubato	flexible tempo with slight variations of speed to enhance musical expression.
scherzando	playful, play in a light-hearted happy manner
schnell	fast
sehr	very
secondo, seconda	second, lower part of a duet
semplice	simple
sempre	always
senza	without
sforzando, sf, sfz	sudden strong accent on a single note or chord
simile	continue in the same manner as has just been indicated
sonore	sonorous, resonant; with rich tone
sopra	above, indicates piano player crossing hands
sostentuto	sustained, play in a prolonged manner
staccato	play short and detached
stringendo	gradually faster, pressing forward
subito	suddenly
tacet	be silent, voice or instrument does not play or sing
tempo	speed at which music is performed
Tempo Primo, Tempo I	return to the original tempo
tranquillo	tranquil, quiet
tre corde	3 strings, release the left pedal on the piano
troppo	too much
tutti	a passage for the whole ensemble
una corda	1 string, depress the left pedal on the piano
vite	fast

vivace   lively, brisk

vivo   lively

volta   time, *prima volta*=1st time, *seconda volta*=2nd time

volti subito, v.s. turn the page quickly

Signs

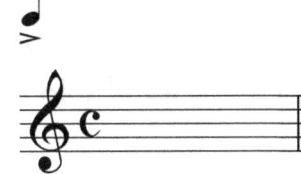 **accent** - a stressed note

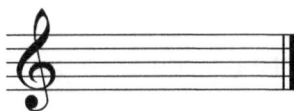 **common time** - symbol for 4/4

 **crescendo** - becoming louder

 **decrescendo** - becoming softer

double bar line - the end of a piece

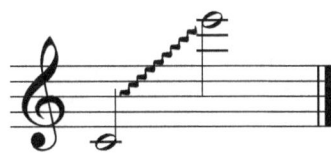 **fermata** - hold note or rest longer than written value

glissando, gliss - a continuous sliding up or down from one pitch to another

 **slur** - play the notes smoothly (legato)

staccato - play short and detached

 **tie** - hold for the combined value of the tied notes

©San Marco Publications 2022

repeat marks - at the second sign go back to the first sign and repeat the music from there. The first sign is left out if the music is repeated from the beginning.

pedal symbol - press/release the right pedal.

tenuto mark - when placed over or under a note, hold it for its full value.

dal segno, D.S. - from the sign.

8va - play one octave higher than written pitch.

8va - play one octave lower than written pitch.

down bow - on a string instrument, play the note by drawing the bow downward.

up bow - on a string instrument, play the note by drawing the bow upward.

breath mark - take a breath or a small break

Terms and Signs

History Recap

Medieval Era (ca 500 - 1450)

Ordo Virtutum (ca. 1151)

Composer: **Hildegard von Bingen** (1098 -1179)

Genre: **morality play** - a drama designed to teach a moral or lesson.

Composed for: **female voices** - the soul, 17 voices portraying the Virtues, the devil, a spoken part for a male voice.

Language: **Latin**

Texture: **monophonic** - a single line of melody without harmony.

Sumer is Icumen In (mid-13th century)

Composer: **Anonymous**

Genre: **Vocal piece** - sung as a round

Composed for: **Six voices**

Texture: **Polyphonic**

Renaissance Era (ca 1450 - 1600)

El Grillo (late 15th century)

Composer: **Josquin des Prez** (1440 -1521)

Genre: **frottola** - secular polyphonic vocal work, ancestor of madrigal

Composed for: **Four voices**

Texture: **Polyphonic**

Global Music

Javanese Gamelan

Composed for: **Gamelan orchestra** - made up of several types of mallet instruments, or keyboard-style instruments struck with mallets or hammers, as well as different drums, flutes, and occasionally stringed instruments or vocalists.

Composer: **No specific composer**. Not traditionally notated. Handed down orally from generation to generation.

Texture: **varies** - repeating melodies (ostinato), strong rhythms, improvisatory

The Raga

Composer: **Traditional Indian music** Based on Indian mode called 'raga,' a scale consisting of varying lengths and often using microtones.

Composed for: at least three, many times more, instruments: **a drone, a drummer**, and **one or more melody instruments**.

Texture: **Highly improvised**

Exam

1. Write the following scales and modes ascending and descending.

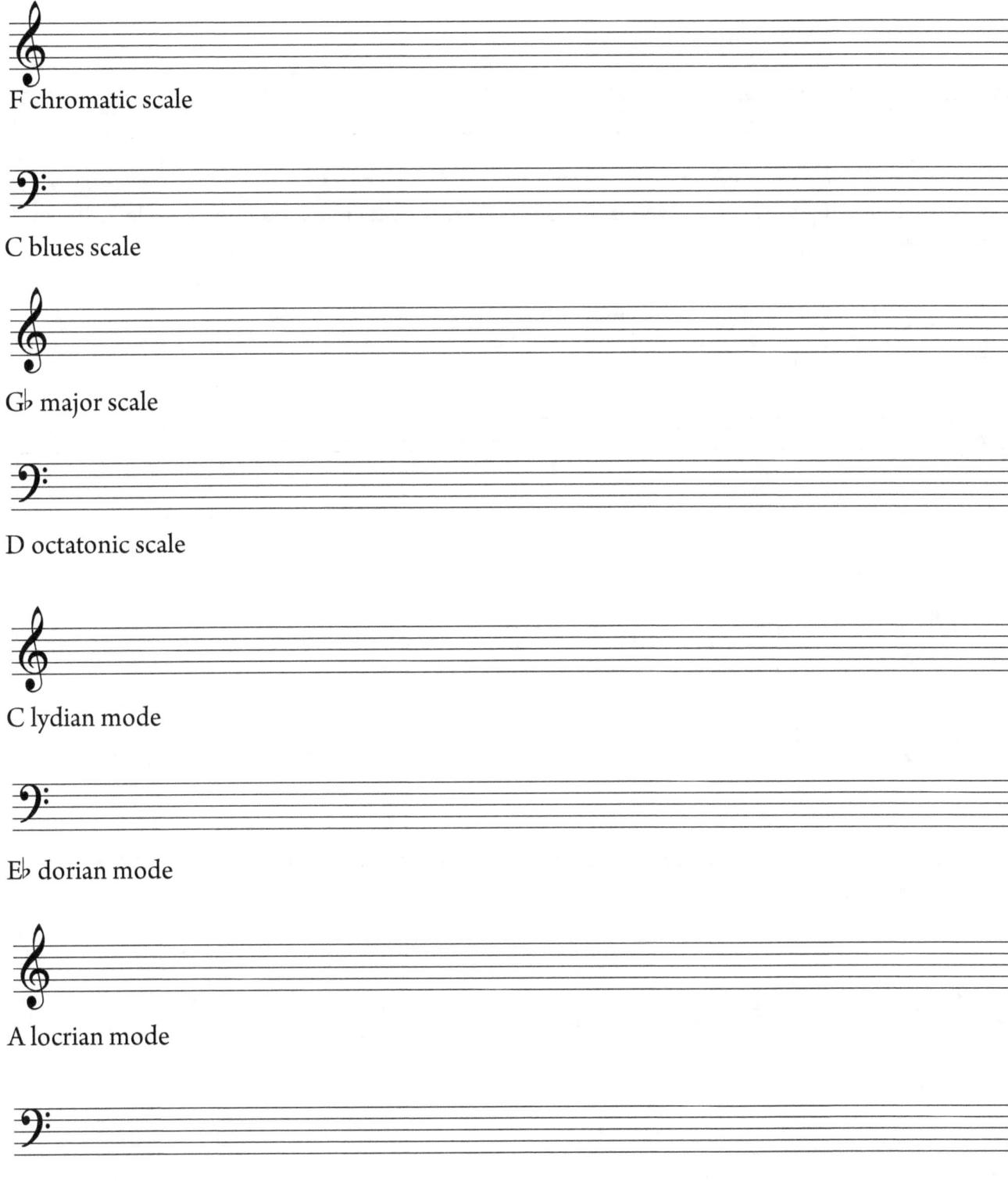

F chromatic scale

C blues scale

G♭ major scale

D octatonic scale

C lydian mode

E♭ dorian mode

A locrian mode

B mixolydian mode

2. Write the following intervals above the given notes. Invert them and rename them.

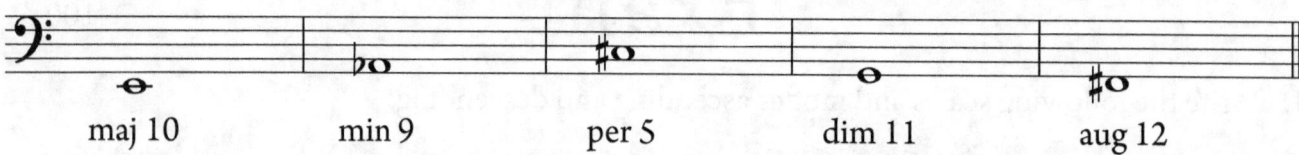

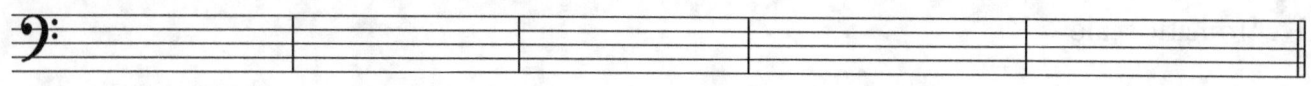

3. For the following phrases: a) Name the key. b) Write a cadence in keyboard style at the end. Name the cadences.

Key:_____   Cadence:_____

Key:_____   Cadence:_____

4. The following melody is written for Horn in F. Name the key. Transpose it to concert pitch. Name the new key.

Antonin Dvorak
Scherzo Capriccioso

Key:_____

Key:_____

___ 5. Name the following chords as: tone cluster, polychord, quartal chord, diminished 7th, dominant 7th, major triad, minor triad, augmented triad or diminished triad.
10

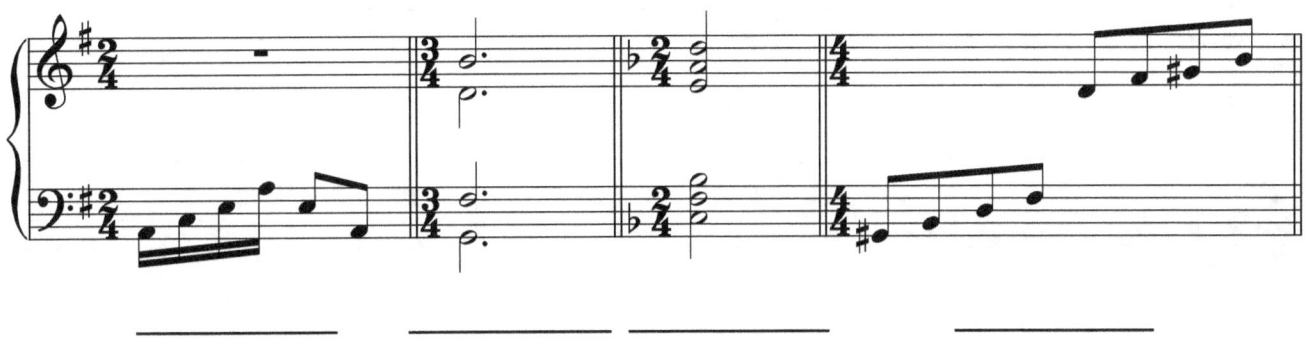

___ 6. For the following melodic fragment:
10
- Name the key.
- Complete the consequent (a) phrase, ending on an unstable scale degree.
- Write an antecedent (b) phrase creating a conrasting period.
- Name each cadence.

Key: _____

5

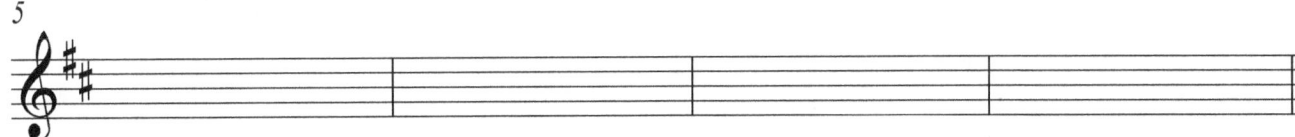

7. Add rests to complete the following measure.

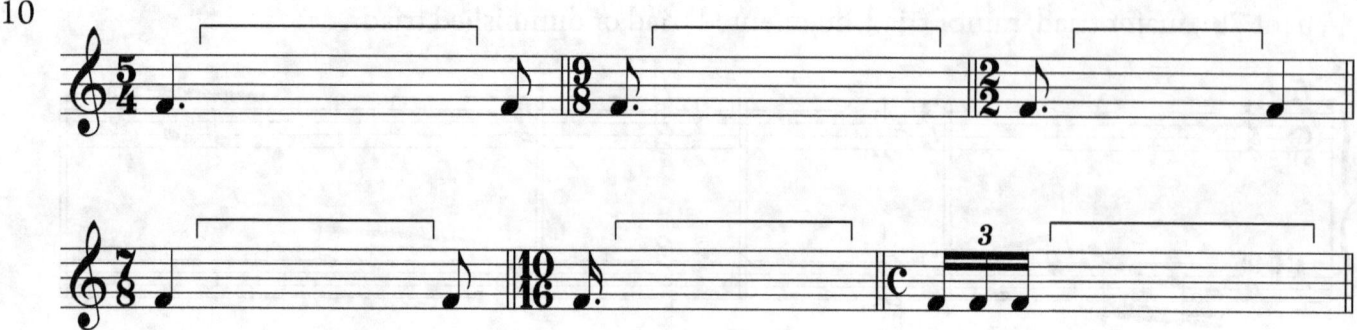

8. Transcribe the following passsage into short score

Giovanni Croce
Is it Nothing to You?

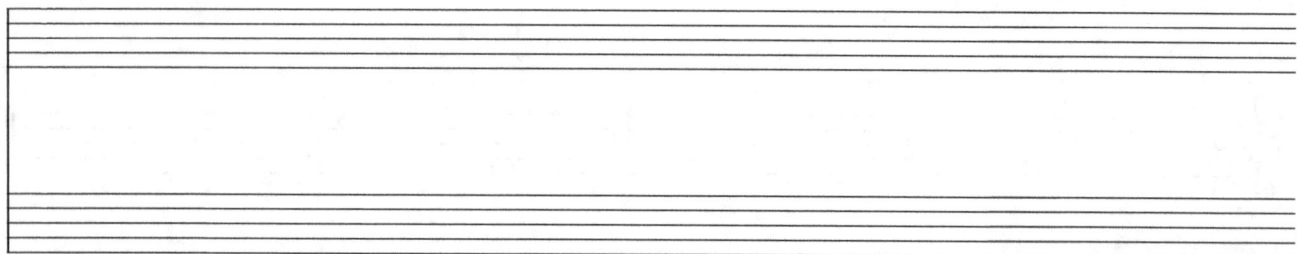

9. Give the best answer to the following statements:

a. an Italian term that means 'suddenly slower.' _____

b. an Indonesian mallet orchestra native to Bali and Java. _____

c. an Italian term that means 'with mute.' _____

d. a mode found in Indian classical music and used in improvised performances. _____

e. the composer of 'El Grillo.' _____

f. a German term meaning 'fast.' _____

g. a single melody without accompaniment. _____

h. a texture where there all parts sing in the same rhythm. _____

i. a French term meaning 'lightly.' _____

j. name for musical era between ca.1450 - 1600. _____

k. the composer of 'Ordo Virtutum.' _____

l. two or more independant melodies singing together. _____

m. a long-necked, guitar-like, string instrument with a gourd shaped resonance chamber used in Indian music. _____

n. a polyphonic vocal work and an ancestor of the madrigal. _____

o. a German term meaning 'slowly.' _____

p. vocal music without instrumental accompaniment. _____

q. a melodic or rhythmic pattern that repeats over and over. _____

r. name for musical era between ca. 500 - 1450. _____

s. means 'clap' and is a rhythmic beat that keeps the time of a raga. _____

t. a single line of modal melody, without a measured rhythm, sung in Latin. _____

10. Answer questions dealing with the following musical excerpt.

Ludwig van Beethoven
String Quartet No.16

a) Name the key of this piece _____

b) Name the enharmonic tonic minor for this key. _____

c) Write the time signature directly on the score.

d) Check two words that describe this time signature:

      ❑simple   ❑duple   ❑compound   ❑triple   ❑quadruple

e) Name the intervals at A: _____ B: _____ C: _____

f) Define **Lento assai**: _____

g) How are mm.7, 8, and 9 related? _____
_____

h) This is an excerpt from a string quartet. What instument is it written for? _____

i) Name the four instruments of the string quartet.

    _____ _____ _____ _____

www.ingramcontent.com/pod-product-compliance
Lightning Source LLC
Chambersburg PA
CBHW081618100526

44590CB00021B/3503